Nothing Concealed

Veiled Secrecy Will Be Brought To Light

by

Jarrod Houston

The contents of this work, including, but not limited to, the accuracy of events, people, and places depicted; opinions expressed; permission to use previously published materials included; and any advice given or actions advocated are solely the responsibility of the author, who assumes all liability for said work and indemnifies the publisher against any claims stemming from publication of the work.

All Rights Reserved
Copyright © 2022 by Jarrod Houston

No part of this book may be reproduced or transmitted, downloaded, distributed, reverse engineered, or stored in or introduced into any information storage and retrieval system, in any form or by any means, including photocopying and recording, whether electronic or mechanical, now known or hereinafter invented without permission in writing from the publisher.

Dorrance Publishing Co
585 Alpha Drive
Pittsburgh, PA 15238
Visit our website at *www.dorrancebookstore.com*

ISBN: 979-8-8852-7411-1
eISBN: 979-8-8852-7525-5

Table of Contents

Preface v
Who Am I 1
Shopping Around 5
Day One 9
Virginia Slims 13
Stun Gun 17
I Am Trouble 23
God? 31
Seay Holler 37
Barbershop 49
Cuz 55
Sex 61
Am I? 65
5-5-5 Video 69
The Hulk 75
It's Our Secret 79
Bare Knuckle 89
I Am Proud of You 93
Homework 97
The Jennings Route 103
Now at Home 107
Coach Scott 115
Glimmer of Hope 121
I Am 129
Peace 135
Standing 141

Preface

The imagery of watching grains of sand slip through one side of the hourglass, is like watching the days of our lives sift away. Our days are fleeting like the sand that seems to be leisurely draining yet is gone in a blink of an eye. The seconds of the sand draining turns to minutes, minutes to hours, and hours to days. Before you realize weeks, months, and years have gone by with opportunities we once dreamed afar distant memory. The looking glass can seem so much larger when staring through it as dreams and aspirations do, but realize that the opportunity is now, so seize the moment.

First and foremost, I would like to thank my Lord and Savior Jesus Christ for guiding my fingers as this book was written. Holy Spirit give me the knowledge, wisdom, and understanding to write honestly, boldly, and from a place of Love. *Nothing Concealed* summed up in one word is Hope. Hope that no matter how your journey starts, it can change for good. Hope, that throughout all the scars that you might have endured from others, forgiveness is within reaching distance.

Writing this book was cathartic. I tried many years ago but was afraid because there were so many accomplished writers in the world but upon deeper thought this book isn't about me, it is for that one person that is battling similar wounds and to finally speak out and gain true liberty.

This is the view through the hourglass of my life from ages four to ten. This book isn't meant to hurt or incriminate anyone but is to help me gain the freedom of releasing all to take the next steps into my future of prosperity. I pray that each person reading this book can gain boldness and do what you have been fearful of for so long, action. In doing, so you might not gain national recognition, or might even shunned but you will accomplish what you have been avoiding for so long, liberation. We were not placed on earth to conform to what society says is "right or wrong" but to lean not on your own understanding and dedicate all your ways to the Lord. I am not a minister but throughout this book you will see how the Lord has covered me from the prayers and blessings from those before me.

The things you will read are going to grip you with fear, anger, hurt, laughter, and sadness, but remember the journey isn't over and you are the captain of your own ship. All the pain endured at a young age taught me that love never fails and forgiveness is real. Own your journey, knowing it isn't over and most importantly OWN WHO YOU ARE.

Who Am I

Mom had this thing, where she manipulated her jaw and lips that would give her away in any hand of poker. She had large white chiclet teeth and something she called the "Goins gap." All the women on her side of the family had it. It was a large, pleasing-to-the-eye gap that told everyone she was a daughter of Gertrude Goins. Along with that gap, you got a few different maneuverings of her jaw that spoke a thousand words to us. Us being her four kids. First was my "young but old-ass actin'" sister Shay, as Mom would always say. Shay defied the rules of a girly girl. With her long, silky flowing curly hair, the beauty pageant daily dress approach she took, and the sass to go along with it, you wouldn't think those big brown eyes accompanied with her pearly whites would be so quick to punch you in the face at any moment. Shay was a live wire that was Mom's assistant. She took her backup mothering role very seriously and made sure we walked the line.

Chonci, the goodie two shoes of the family that could do no wrong but always seemed to be vicariously living through my dumb decisions, was the people's choice. Small in stature but large in heart, many people would say, because there wasn't a door he wouldn't hold open until the last person or a good deed he wouldn't do for others outside the family. I admired him for his shapeshifter ability to impress the onlookers, but I didn't dare wear those hideous adult dress-up clothes he adorned himself in for the endorsements of adults but the jeering of his fellow classmates. Chonci forced himself into a leadership position that only he wanted and no one else cared about.

Halston aka Scooter, "the baby," who—never seeming have been detached from the umbilical cord—was always on Momma's hip. Scooter got handed the pretty gene of the family: long, flowing curly hair and a complexion that was a crowd stopper anyplace we went. He was Mom's prized possession. She admired the *oooos* and *ahhhhs* more than he did and would have her Goins gap shining bright whenever people would stop to comment on how beautiful he was.

That left me: the odd ball. I inherited those large Goins teeth minus the gap, but they didn't suit me so well, while also having to carry around ears that stuck out like small teacups on the side of my head. One of my ears looked like someone took a bite out of it or, as Shay would say, "your earlobe is doing the peace sign." I also sported permanently swollen cheeks as though I had been stung by a nest of hornets. Dad said I looked like a dick with a bald head, ears sticking out, swollen cheeks, with a teeny-tiny frame. I didn't fit like a lost puzzle piece in the wrong box, and I accepted it with every glance at my siblings.

Back to Mom and her many maneuverings…the first was the tooth-sucking noise. First, Mom would open her mouth wide, move her tongue to the left side of her mouth, slide her tongue up to the tooth beside her canine, drop one side of her mouth as though she were having a stroke, and begin to suck. This noise was repulsing and damn near infuriating. This was her point—to alarm us like a mother animal in the wild that she's about to jump stupid on us if we didn't adjust what the hell we were doing. I got this alert call more often than any of the others because I seemed to always be doing "sumtin'."

The second mouth maneuver was the "I'm at my damn wits' end with you." This usually happened in the store. It came after the pep talk, before entering the store. The pep talk went something like this, "Don't touch shit, don't ask for shit, because I ain't buying you shit."

Not thirty seconds upon entering the store, I would get Alzheimer's and forget the pep talk. Enamored with all the impulse-buying items at the front of the store, my hands would dig through items like a dog digging for a bone. That's when she would snarl like a pit bull showing her big chiclet teeth, bite down hard so you could see her cheek muscles and tighten her lip up so much that it created a megaphone. From there, she would lean in so close I could smell her Mom breath and loudly whisper, arousing every shoppers' ears in the next two aisles, enunciating every single angry syllable, "DIDN'T. I. TELL. YOUR. STUPID. ASS. NOT. TO. ASK. FOR. OR. TOUCH. SHIT!"

It wasn't the words that scared the ever-loving Jesus out of me but her delivery. She meant more than business and it was on! I would give that fearful shiver and prepare myself for the inevitable slap.

You never knew where the slap was landing but you had better known two things before receiving it: you better not block it and you had better not even think about moving. I got my stand-still slap with the direct threat of, "You better suck it up or I'll really give you something to cry about later!" With the three of us boys, this was a situation that always played out like *Groundhog Day*.

Mom's third of many fascial maneuvers was the look of uncertainty. Mom wore her emotions on her sleeve like the old watch she always wore that never seemed to tick or tock. She would kind of scan a room, tuck in her bottom lip, and bring that top lip tight to cover the bottom one, as if it were a comforter lying on top of a bed sheet. Many times, this face would come on weekends when she was leaving for work, knowing we were there to fend for ourselves with the guidance of Shay. She would kiss us, tuck that top lip, inhale and exhale deeply as though she knew there was no other choice. We were getting older and more daring to defy the rules and roles of the house. Mom and Dad had to make a decision to shop around for someone to watch us.

Shopping Around

Blue-collared hard-working parents, Mom and Dad always seemed to be behind on bills like David Justice in the batter's box for the Atlanta Braves; scratching tooth and nail to get a hit to provide.

Four siblings, all of which are too young to monitor each other let alone themselves, put my parents at a crossroads: do you work to pay for childcare, does Mom stay at home, or do you use the neighborhood recommended "affordable" babysitter? Being the overly protective mother she was, Mom did her Google search reviews with word of mouth. She talked to other moms who had used local babysitters in the area before deciding to do a home visit with the most highly recommended one.

To me, the first day's inspection didn't go well. For starters, the moth ball smell had me holding my breath like when riding over a long bridge. Then I had to climb the termite-infested steps, make a swift lateral step to avoid falling through the rotted boards that were littered with holes, and approach the front raggedy door that looked like it was from *The Addams Family*. That was more than enough to turn around and run for our lives, but it was obvious Mom was mentally trying to make lemonade out of lemons—hell, rotten lemons at that. Eyes focused forward, Mom said nothing. She inhaled deeply as though her nose had become accustomed to the rancid moth ball smell and gave two hard blows to the heavy worn door. The old ragtag door responded back with two echoed slams back from Mom's knuckles.

No answer; the lady had to know we were coming but maybe it was a game of anticipation to make it seem as though she were extremely busy tending to the other children. Or she was just fat and old. Upon answering the door, she looked as weather-beaten and broken down as her door.

"Hello. I am Kathy and these are my boys."

The lady's voice was deep and raspy. "Nice to meet you all. Come on in."

I was overcome so much by the snickering monster that I couldn't remember her name. I just knew I had better not laugh in this woman's face or hell would be awaiting me.

Because I couldn't hear her name, the only fitting name for her was "The Lady." By default, ma'am was the right way to address her anyway. I knew better than to address her with nothing else except *Yes, ma'am* or *No, ma'am*, or that would've been my ass when I got home. How Mom would even know or find out, I wasn't sure, but I wasn't going to try it because Mom had a sense wittier than a cat on its ninth life.

"The Lady" was an older Black lady that had an upstanding name in the community because she was pastor of a local church in our area and watched a couple other kids that we knew in passing. I wondered how she could be a pastor because I used to always hear, "cleanliness is next to godliness." If that were the case, then this house was the gates to Hell and the lady was the mumu-wearing gatekeeper.

The Lady probably thought I was very respectful because I didn't take my eyes off her, but only due to the black thingies protruding out of her neck and the smell of cheap cocoa butter. That must have been the rite of passage in that house, to slap slop cheap liquidy cocoa butter everywhere, because the smell radiated from every direction. Maybe the cocoa butter numbed your nose to any other smells, like the moth balls that reeked in the front flower bed or the distinct smell of the rotting wood on the porch. Either way, my nose was a cocktail of smells that subliminally resounded DO NOT ENTER.

Mom wore the outfit of solidarity like I had to during the Pledge of Allegiance at school. A look where she nodded her head with her fake half smile that she only revealed during times of uncomfortable talks with other adults. Mom ignored all the signs to grab us and run away to make herself feel comfortable about entering The Lady's house and to accept the fact her babies were going to stay here.

The Lady was big-boned as Mom would say, but I knew she was just fat. She was sloppy and anytime I remember her, she had on a mumu, never seemed to wear a bra, and her breasts looked like large sandbags that hung down to her

Nothing Concealed: Veiled Secrecy Will Be Brought To Light

bellybutton. She was who she was from the very beginning, and maybe that was endearing to Mom. Her breath didn't smell bad, but I knew the smell of Aim toothpaste with baking soda, and she reeked of it when she spoke.

After the first impression of the house and The Lady, Mom had to be hesitant, but you could tell she was desperate. When Mom was nervous or unsure about something she would talk out loud, questioning and answering herself. We sat in The Lady's driveway in the car as Mom had a two-way conversation with herself.

Mumbling to herself, "Who else is this close? I can get here quickly if need be. She seemed okay, but that house was rough."

Mom took a minute as though she was allowing time for the other person in her head to think on the questions.

"Nobody, Kathy. The next closest is Morristown. I can get here in fifteen minutes. Yes, her house was not the best, but I feel like my babies will be okay until we find something else."

Then, The Lady closed the deal. She had talked about feeding us meals throughout the day but the official deal closer was when she talked about how she disciplined, or as Mom would say it, "minding." We were three boys very close in age and very impressionable, so there had to be structure and discipline in the house. Upon a simple glance of inspection throughout the house from the living room vantage point, nothing seemed too alarming to Mom and, with her third look, slightly hunched over back and tightly covered lips, Mom agreed for us to be babysat five days a week.

The Lady's house was unforgettable for a few reasons: the pungent smell of moth balls and cocoa butter, the sticky floor breeding grounds of the cockroaches, and the heavy shadow that jumped on my back when I entered that white raggedy craftsman-style home on day one.

Day One

A dark and gloomy aura lay dormant in the lady's house when my siblings and I walked into the house on day one. What did we know about dark and gloomy? We just knew Mom and Dad told us we had better behave or there'd be enough ass whoopings to go around for days. That is all we needed to hear, so the first two weeks, we were quiet as mice.

My nose had to adjust to her house smell: mildewed carpet from the lack of a place mat at the front door, moth balls, and the staleness of leftover food. I was a connoisseur of such and was well-versed in the stench of leftovers. At home, Mom cooked with reused lard and the smell of days-old Crisco danced through the air from the kitchen, permeating throughout the house. My educated hypothesis of the putrid smell that lingered due to leftovers was: never having a true Glad lock container and only using Country Crock butter containers with aluminum foil as the lid. There was no locking in of smells in those containers, so the house reeked of cross-contaminating leftovers. You could identify what type of food was cooked just by smelling the container and, to top it off, the hint of baking soda wafted every time the refrigerator door swung open as it sat smack dab in the middle of the fridge.

As I became numbed to the smell, things started to slowly change during the third week at The Lady's house.

I started noticing more foot traffic coming in and out, not staying long but maybe fifteen to twenty minutes at a time. In those days, I was appointed watchman by Dad, which meant I was always on guard, analyzing the situation like a junkyard dog. I was all bark and no bite—being undersized; all I had was my quick-witted sarcastic remarks that more than likely The Lady would soon find out about.

My head lay on a scratchy pillow on a sheet that was placed on the ground in front of the TV. We all lay at ground zero beneath the smells of the house. I couldn't sleep and was fidgeting with Jimmy legs. Tossing and turning, trying to find the right head groove in that itchy pillow, I heard The Lady call out to me with a very soft and soothing voice.

"Jarrod."

I don't know how I heard her, but Mom had this skill as well that allowed her to whisper during times of total chaos that came across like a roaring lioness.

Her voice carried from the first bedroom, which was nestled to the right of the front door. Everyone else was fast asleep on their sheets and all I knew was to respond.

"Ma'am?" I asked inquisitively, mimicking her tone so as not to wake anyone up.

"Come in here, baby."

"Yes, ma'am."

Upon standing, I could feel the shaggy mildewed-smelling rug under my feet as I baby-stepped quietly towards the room. Her voice was tucked away in the corner of the room, and the sun shining ever so slightly through the curtains helped guide me to her sitting on the edge of the bed.

I reluctantly went to her. Standing a few feet away from her dark silhouette, "Yes, ma'am, you called me?"

"Jarrod, come here," she whispered even more quietly, as to entice me to come closer so I could hear her.

My thoughts are swirling. Why aren't my brothers and sister here with me? Why did she just call me? Did I do something wrong? Why is the room so dark? What should I do?

"Jarrod," she said, so low that I had to lip read through the sunlight and shadows to make sure it was my name.

"Jarrod."

I leaned in to hear her more clearly. She reached her dark, swollen, almost puffy hand through the shadows and grabbed my wrist. Her hand cut through the beams of sun like a shadowy knife. It was the type of black you could still see in the dimmed room but dark enough that if it moved swiftly, you would lose track because your eyes would have to adjust.

Gently grabbing my wrist, she pulled me in like Mom would, but it was different. Her voice was soft and inviting like Mom's, but there was something else there. I stepped in closer to her...so close I could smell the cheap smell of Aim toothpaste and feel her loose breast against my cheek. Pulling me even closer to her, the heaviness of her breast consumed my head.

She took my wrist and guided it to one of her loose breasts. "Squeeze, Jarrod."

Fear ran through my veins—but I do as I'm told and never question an adult.

Her voice got softer, but I could feel her breath on my forehead and the cadence of her breathing up. "Squeeze harder."

I did as I'm told and squeezed as hard as I could. Her mumu and breast overflowed between my fingers like Playdoh.

Taking my other hand into hers, she guided it until I reached the tethered end of her . I couldn't move. I was a puppet on the strings getting manipulated by the puppet master. She manipulated my hand by turning my wrist face up and slowly lifted her mumu.

She felt me starting to tense up but then reassured me with, "It's okay." I relaxed slightly and then my hand was consumed in warm, hairy swollenness. She pressed my hand deeper.

"Good job, Jarrod. You're doing a good job."

My hands were at her mercy. Time was frozen while my hands squeezed and stroked at her strings.

I must have been doing a good job because she is saying how proud she is of me. In an instant, she pulls me in close, kisses me on the forehead, and tells me to go lay back down while she wipes my hand with the bottom of her mumu.

"Don't wake the other babies. I am proud of you, Jarrod."

"Yes, ma'am."

Virginia Slims

Family is all you have, and that is ingrained in you where I am from. "Blood is thicker than water" is what I've heard family members say multiple times throughout my life.

What if family hurts you the same way strangers do? What do you do or say? Nothing?

My cousin was five years older than me and was what others would call the "bad kid." No father in his life and a mother that let him come and go as he pleased. I looked up to him because he was a rebel. He didn't care to cuss out a teacher or flip off a car passing by, and that's how I felt, too. But I knew to stay in line or there would be hell to pay. I looked up to him so much that one time he got me to steal a pack of Virginia Slims from Mamaw's purse. To impress him, I smoked, or at least tried to smoke, one behind a dumpster until Mom caught us.

"Jarrod, what the hell are y'all doing? Answer me." We stood silent.

"Y'all had better not be doing what I think y'all are doing."

Maybe it was her stealth-like Momma mode that caught me by surprise or my lack of smoking experience, but I began to choke on that Virginia Slim, and it gave us away.

"You are doing what I thought, damnit, Jarrod!" Being the rebel he was, I thought my cousin would say, "Yes, I'm smoking and what you gonna do about it," but it was the opposite. I mean the complete opposite. He just stood, feet rooted in the ground, holding in the long drag he just pulled off the Slim, and said, "Yes, ma'am."

I was floored. All the run-ins with the cops, principals, and teachers, and all this guy had to say was, "Yes, ma'am." I became terrified because I saw the fear on my cousin's face, and we both knew the type of woman my mom was.

Mom's parenting of three young boys was, let's just say, unorthodox. She was the evil villain we all loved and knew it was a slippery slope to a slap at any moment we decided to get out of line. My cousin's onset paralysis and my cough behind that project dumpster was all she needed to release the kraken.

"Okay, so you want to be grown like Mamaw, I see." Never looking at my cousin, I smelled the fear on him like the old food and baby diaper stench coming from the project dumpster. I took my opportunity to flex for my cousin. In my toughest coughing voice, cocking my head to the side, and squinting, "Yes, ma'am."

"Yes, ma'am," she repeated, as if to not believe I just challenged her. I braced my feet for the wind-up slap, but nothing came. This moment was like when a dog senses fear and starts to chase, so we both stood paralyzed from the waist down. Planted, feet firm, I prepared for the inevitable, but still nothing came.

"Okay, Jarrod, you want to be grown? Hand me those cigs."

I handed them over because I won, and she knew it. My cousin was obviously concerned because he stood there frozen, not making any sudden movements, keeping his eyes locked on her. Mom began to pack the slims by firmly gripping the pack in one hand and then striking them on the heel of her opposite hand. For Mom to have never smoked, she did this with the confidence of someone with trained experience. She packed for what felt like a lifetime. During this time, she was obviously mentally critiquing her plan. Then it happened. She changed her tone and commanded my cousin, "Back up! You wanna to be a tough guy, so you gonna to sit and watch."

Me not knowing what's about to happen, I adjust to see him.

"Here, you idiot!" She hands me the slims and says, "Smoke!"

"Okay." I cough my way through the first slim like it's nothing. I kind of look at her side eyed. She clenches her jaws together and then I realize...I messed up. Talking through her teeth, "Smoke!" I take another and gag and cough through the second slim.

My cousin starts to squirm. "You sit your ass still and watch!"

"Yes, ma'am."

"Jarrod, SMOKE!" I grab another, take a long drag from the slim, and throw up.

"Mom, PLEASE."

Nothing Concealed: Veiled Secrecy Will Be Brought To Light

"Jarrod, SMOKE!" She grabs the pack, removes two, puts them in my mouth, and lights them. "SMOKE!"

Begging and pleading, "Mom, PLEASE, I CAN'T."

"JARROD, SMOKE!"

I double barreled these two, coughing, spitting up, and crying. She didn't care. She grabbed my cousin by his arm, pulled him close.

"WATCH JARROD SMOKE!"

She handed me another two slims and said, "You have two minutes to smoke them or I'm bustin' your ASS!" Two minutes never felt so long, but I threw my way up through the rest of those slims.

Mom looked at both of us. "Do you want the rest of these to smoke?" My cousin, with tears in his eyes and me looking like I came out of the gas chamber, simultaneously, "No, ma'am."

"That's what the hell I thought!" She dropped the pack of slims in front of us and walked off, daring us to pick them back up.

I looked at my cousin and then down at those slims. With tears in my eyes and snot running from every crevice, I kicked those damn slims as hard as I could. The carton flew down into the stinky creek below. I walked off, congested and defeated.

Even with my cousin's fearful hesitancy to help me, he understood me, and I wanted to be just like big cuz.

Stun Gun

Sitting on a sleigh bed was always so difficult since I was shorter than your average eight-year-old. I would have to grab as high as I could with one arm, gripping onto the comforter that was covered with designs of oversized flowers, before hiking my opposite leg up to find the slight lip of the sleigh bed. Once I had that positioning, I would take a few bounces on the leg that was on the ground to gain momentum and give it my all to hoist myself onto the bed. Usually, I would get into a half-straddle position, like a cowboy sideways on a horse. From there, it was all brute strength. I would huff and puff, squirming around until I got both knees on the plateau of the bed. Once on the bed, I would flip to my back and scootch to the edge so I could dangle my feet. With my feet dangling, Chonci would either try the same technique, since he was even shorter than me, or would use my foot as a live rope to hoist himself up.

Any time Dad would have us in his room and Mom stationed in her comfort zone of the kitchen, it was for learning purposes.

"Boys, if you don't mind then it don't matter," Dad would say as he was scanning the room, connecting eyes, to make sure we were focused on the lesson at hand.

"What does that mean, Dad?" I asked with my feet dangling off the bed like live worms on a hook.

"In life, there will be times you want to quit because the pain is so bad, but if you don't mind the pain, then you can push through and reach your goal. Most people give up because the pain is unbearable. If you can learn to enjoy the pain, then you can learn to push past your potential and tap into your capabilities."

Not knowing what he is talking about, Chonci and I would still shake our heads in total agreement.

"Boys, there are rewards for those that push past their pain threshold."

Dad takes a moment for us to let things soak in, but I was too busy seeing how fast I could swing my legs back and forth off the edge of the sleigh bed cliff.

I see Dad reach down into the closet. When he stood up, he was holding a small black rectangle with two pieces of metal on each side. Dad examined it for a few minutes before opening the bottom of the rectangle. A nine-volt battery fell out. Dad examined it again, made sure it was secured back in place, then closed the bottom of the rectangle. He flipped it around a few times, switching hands, like he was checking to see if it were weighted correctly. Finally, he chose to hold it in his right hand. Upon choosing his right hand, he slid his thumb up the side, where a black button stuck out. "Look close at this, boys. It can hurt you if you don't use it correctly."

Curious, I asked, "What is it?"

"Son, it's called a stun gun."

"A what?"

At that time, Dad moved it closer to our faces and pressed the button. A lightning bolt jumped quickly from one of the metal pieces to the other and made a *POP POP POP POP* sound. I jumped back on the bed and my legs stiffened with fear.

"Dad, what is that for?"

"It is a self-defense weapon that people carry to protect themselves."

"Why do you have it?"

"Just in case."

"Just in case, what?"

Holding the button longer this time, *POP POP POP POP POP POP POP* as the lightning danced back and forth on the metal knobs sticking out.

"Boys, I want to teach you how to control yourselves during pain and to push through. I told you there's a reward for those that can push past their pain threshold."

Dad started tossing the stun gun back and forth in his hands looking at us, almost as if he were trying to tease us. The stun gun's toss from palm to palm hypnotized me. My eyes became fixated on it, like a cat chasing a laser. I was so entranced, I forgot what Dad was even saying. Realizing it, Dad stopped, pressed the button, and the *POP POP POP POP* shook me from my trance.

All I could reply was, "Yes, sir."

With that last electrical burst of the stun gun, I erupted in fear but couldn't show Dad. My palms become sweaty, heart racing, and thoughts overcoming my mind.

Is Dad trying to kill us?

What did I do?

This is going to hurt so bad!

Is the lightning going to burn my skin?

I was ready to scream for Mom, but I didn't know what would happen. My mind was about to explode with screams of horror.

Right when it felt like my skin was crawling with bugs, Dad spoke up. "Well, if you are tough enough, I will pay you a dollar for each time you let me stun gun you."

"Dad, I don't know. Is it going to hurt?"

Without hesitation, Dad replied, "Yes, but if you don't mind then it don't matter."

Chonci and I glanced at each other reluctantly.

As he pulls out an old wrinkly dollar, "Who's going to go first?"

Draping my head, looking at Chonci out of the corner of my eye, Dad repeats, "Who's going first?"

I didn't want to go at all, but I didn't want to disappoint Dad. My palms became moist again and all I could do was pray to myself, "Please just let Dad go away. Please Lord. Please."

And then Chonci spoke up. "I will, Dad."

Dad waited for a moment. I could feel him staring at me, but I didn't want to look up and meet eye-to-eye. "Jarrod, I want you to earn this dollar."

Defeated and head hung low, all I could say in my broken voice was a "Yes, sir."

"Son, where do you want me to stun gun you? I can just try on your leg first, so you can see what it feels like." I said nothing but nod my head yes in agreement.

Knowing that if I showed how terrified I was and started crying, I would've gotten whipped and then stun gunned anyway, I chose the plight of the stun gun instead.

I became overcome with tunnel vision. Everything in the room became a blurry painting, except Dad's hand and the stun gun that was resting in it.

My stomach started quivering with butterflies and I felt cold, but my hands were sweaty. I wanted to scream, "STOP, DAD. I DON'T WANT TO DO THIS," but I was more worried that I would disappoint him for not manning up.

Dad leaned down slowly and looked me in the eyes.

"Jarrod, learn to embrace the pain, because it's temporary."

All I could do was bite down, clenching my jaw as hard as I could. I didn't want to look but Dad said, "Jarrod. Pay attention."

Voice quivering with fear but knowing there was nowhere to run, "Yes, sir."

I look up as he is placing the two metal prongs on my right thigh. We lock eyes.

"Count to three, Jarrod."

"*One.*" *POP POP POP POP.*

The pain was paralyzing. I could feel the lightning bolt shoot through my thigh, gripping and squeezing my muscle as it traveled back and forth to the metal prongs. I bit down, clenching my teeth as hard as I could, but the lightning took control of my body. My leg flew in the air, and I fell back on the bed. I wanted to cry but couldn't. Looking at Dad, the only thing my body would allow me to do was wince and let out a painful gurgle.

The pain blanketed me like the coldest cold I'd ever felt. My fingers burned and tingled like they were simultaneously frostbitten and being submerged in hot water. My feet felt like I stomped repeatedly on a bed of needles and my muscles went into a rigor mortis state. It felt like a full body cramp.

I started to cry and all I could hear Dad say was, "Suck it up. If you don't mind, it don't matter. And I only held it there for a second."

All I could do was dry my tears up immediately and rub my thigh back and forth like you do when you hit your pinky toe on the corner of the couch.

With a laugh, "Good job, son," and he threw me the wrinkled dollar.

Chonci perked up and asked, "Did it hurt, Jarrod?"

I looked at Dad first before giving my answer and sheepishly said, "Kinda."

"Jarrod, it didn't hurt. I only touched you for maybe a second."

"Are you ready, Chonci?"

"Yes, sir."

"I am going to touch your shoulder with it."

"Okay, Dad."

There was no countdown. Chonci looked at Dad as though he had something to prove and bit his lip. Dad squeezed the button and *POP POP POP POP* jumped the lightning bolts as he jammed it on Chonci's shoulder.

It threw Chonci back on the bed as well, but instead of crying, Chonci started doing his weird laugh. Chonci has this one laugh that he always does when he is hurt but tries to cover it up. It's a mixture of a slight whimper and a scary high-pitch clown laugh.

I even winced when watching Chonci, but I couldn't let him beat me, especially since he looked at me with that "I'm tougher than you" look he always did.

"I'm ready to go again, Dad."

"Are you sure? You almost cried last time."

The entire time I was talking to Dad, I was side-eyeing Chonci so he could see me. "I won't even flinch, Dad."

Dad took the stun gun, flipped it back to his dominant hand, and thrusted it into my left shoulder. I bit down, not showing any pain, and this seemed to excite Dad because he left it on my shoulder even longer. It felt like five minutes, and right before I broke down, he jerked it off my shoulder.

"Great job, Jarrod! That's how you embrace the pain."

Chonci didn't give me any time to revel in my victory. "Let's go, Dad."

Dad made a quick pivot with a smile on his face and placed the stun gun on Chonci's stomach and squeezed. I could tell this hurt because Chonci had a blank, focused stare so he wouldn't cry.

Even more excited, "Way to focus, Chonci!"

Looking right at me, Chonci slightly nodded, and I knew there was only one thing to do.

Pointing to my stomach, "Dad, I'm ready."

He pivoted back and, without any hesitation, placed the stun gun on my stomach and squeezed. It made my abs flex like I had done one thousand sit-ups. The pain radiated up my spine to the top of my head, but I knew I couldn't show it. I stood knowing I wasn't going to break. When Dad let go of the trigger, he looked impressed. "Dang. Good job, Jarrod."

It turned into a nonstop stun gunning meat tenderizing seminar. Chonci would go, and then I would ante up. This went on until we heard some scuffling coming down the hall. It was obviously Mom because the wood floor creaked louder when she walked due to her "flat footedness," as Dad would say. Also, she was easily identified because of all the snap, crackle, and popping her ankles did with every step.

Mom must've heard one of us wincing because the crackling of her ankles came to an abrupt halt.

"MARVIN, WHAT ARE Y'ALL DOIN' IN THERE?" We all three paused and looked at each other, but Dad seemed unbothered. So, we continued, and right as Dad turned to me, Mom appeared in the doorway snarling, showing all her pearly whites.

"MARVIN, WHAT IN GOD'S NAME ARE YOU DOING?"

"KATHY, shut up."

"I CAN NOT BELIEVE YOU ARE SITTING IN HERE STUN GUNNING MY BABIES."

"They need to learn how to handle pain."

Shaking her head in disgust, "Not like this. NIP THIS SHIT IN THE BUD, RIGHT NOW!"

Whenever Mom said "nip it in the bud," we all knew it was hell to pay if we didn't.

I could tell Dad was about to explode, so I jumped up and waved my money in the air with pure jubilation in my voice, "Momma, I won ten dollars and Chonci only got eight."

Tilting her head, Mom smirked, only revealing slight disgust with Dad and the situation. "Well, good job, but this better not happen again."

I wave my ten dollars in the air as I stroll out of the room, making sure to look Chonci in the eyes because I knew a gut punch was awaiting me later anyways.

I Am Trouble

In a small rural country town where your brother is only eleven months older than you and your sister is five years older, every teacher has a preconceived thought of how you should or shouldn't be. With me, that notion was made worse by my older sister and brother being angels. They never got a red card, sat out at recess, got sent to the principal, or had to stand out in the hall for disruptions. Every teacher I had would always say, "Jarrod, you are not like your sister and brother." I even had a teacher tell me that she wished I was my brother multiple times throughout the years. Because I was battling inner demons that I didn't even know I wasn't supposed to have, I believed what my coaches, teachers, and everyone else had to say and accepted I was trouble. I started wearing trouble like a tailored suit. The only person that seemed to want me was Mamaw Gerty. Mamaw was a key fixture in my life, but she was like the saying "so close but yet so far away."

She only lived fifteen minutes away, but we would only see her sporadically and, when we did, Mom would act as though she was on *Supermarket Sweeps*. *Supermarket Sweeps* was a show that helped me not hurt as I imagined winning money for knowing where groceries were throughout the store by finding items faster than your opponents. Mamaw was an old but young grandmother. Walking into her house was like a Heilig-Meyers furniture store display. The dark brown coffee table reeked of old hard candies that were strategically placed in the middle of the table. I would always open up that glass lid knowing that all that candy would be stuck together but hoping there would be one loose one to suck on during our brief visits. The love seat had gold waterfall lights hanging over the back of it with three out of the five lights out; two dark brown side tables had lamps sitting on them that were never plugged up and probably didn't even have light bulbs in them; two accent chairs sat catty-cornered, slightly facing in towards the centerpiece coffee table; the oval rug was underneath the table that had the same colors to help the room flow; and last but not least, the china cabinet sat in the far corner wall. This was a massive dark wood glass cased monstrosity that was all eye candy. You knew that when you came into Mamaw's house you had better not get one fingerprint on it, and don't even think about using the expensive chinaware that was inside. To me, it was a huge paperweight, but Mom always commented how beautiful it was on the trips there. Mamaw was a movie-like character with all her sayings and interactions with various people that I noticed when I was there.

"Jarrot, Jarrot," she yelled to me from the back bedroom.

"Ma'am?"

"Get your ass back here."

"Yes, ma'am."

I ran to the back and could hear what sounded like maracas. I slowly stick my head around the corner, peeping my head into the room and Mamaw is shaking a pill bottle. "Get in here, Jarrot." I walk into the room, and Mamaw is sitting high up on the edge of that chalet bed and her side table is lined with what seemed like a thousand pill bottles.

Mamaw, looking at me and shaking a bottle, says, "I pay the cost to be the boss," and hands me a crisp hundred-dollar bill. "Take this and give it to your dumb momma."

I chuckle and take it because how could Mamaw also know Mom was dumb? At that moment someone else walks in the room and says, "Gerty?" She picks up another bottle, inspects it by shaking it around, opens it, and hands the unknown person some pills. He digs in his pocket and hands her some wadded-up cash and scrambles out of the house. I didn't know what was going on, but I wanted to pay the cost to be the boss. Mamaw was revered by the young and old and maybe it was because of the power she had in her hand: pills. Mamaw was always sickly, in and out of the hospital, but I knew of her as the only woman construction worker during her time. Maybe it was her being around all those men that made her become so hard and create this persona of Scarface that no one wanted to dare cross her, or maybe it was just who she was born to be. Because of this reverence she had, I looked up to her.

Nothing Concealed: Veiled Secrecy Will Be Brought To Light

Standing there in awe, she asked, "You want to live with me? Because you always been my pick." I didn't know how to respond so I just stared and waited for what she had to say next. "How's your crazy-ass Daddy? I should've killed him the first time I shot him."

Still standing there in total silence I had nothing to say but wanted to scream yes to moving in with her and living the life she lived and yes to she should have killed him the first time she shot Dad. I knew Mamaw felt differently towards me because she would always voice it when I saw her. Maybe it was that I looked more like the Goins side of the family or that she could feel how our rebellious spirits harmonized together whenever we were in the same room. Either way, I always felt wanted with Mamaw Gert and knew she felt wanted around me, no matter how short the interactions we had.

It always seemed like we were at the store, so *Supermarket Sweeps* just helped me utilize the day-to-day shopping my mom did. Maybe the store was Mom's happy place, but, damn, we were always there. Fridays would be our large shopping days where my brothers and I would first get the talk about not touching shit and then have to create a leash with our arm by holding on the top plastic corner piece of the shopping cart. I would imagine those plastic pieces as bumpers for the chaotic shoppers bumping into each other to reach for the last can of peas. This never happened but would have made all of our shopping days all the more enjoyable. Your arm bet not come off that buggy or you would get the quickest slap from any angle Mom had created with her varied ways of moving the buggy: behind, besides, or the front pull. Even though we had the large shopping day on Fridays, Mom would whisk us away almost daily because she forgot something to add into the same routine "specialty" meals weekly.

Monday - spaghetti

Tuesday - chili

Wednesday - goulash

Thursday – toss up day because Mom might actually try to follow a recipe

Friday - homemade pizza

Saturday morning - gravy-n-biscuits

Sunday was a "you never know but shut up and eat" day, with the occasional visits to the China House Restaurant.

How the hell can you forget chili seasoning every Tuesday, or pizza sauce and pineapples every Friday for that homemade pizza you made with the oversized pineapples on there? She never asked if we liked them but did her second facial maneuver if we complained, talking through her gritted teeth, letting me know how she didn't have to cook shit and that I had better pick around those pineapples and shut the hell up. Mom was so hard but loved us even harder. That was just her saying she cared without saying it, so, begrudgingly, I ate those huge can-cut pineapples so much I grew to love them. Weekly, our days were littered with spontaneous trips to the store with threats of not asking for or touching anything. These home-away-from-home trips allowed me to memorize the blueprint of the stores Mom shopped at—Save-a-lot, Walmart, Wholesale Food Outlet, Winn Dixie, and Piggly Wiggly—and also helped me see the interactions of other kids in the store. These moments intrigued me when it came to interactions with the older kids. Older kids had more of a say so or didn't care about talking back or arguing with their parents in any aisle of the store. Because of this, I began to sneak around and hang with the older kids on my block and bus.

Learning to cuss was my first accomplishment. I could say every word in the book but never dared take the Lord's name in vain. It was something about talking grown but knowing when too far had been reached. "I cuss like a sailor, but I don't f'in sink the ship," Mom would say in justifying her profound heart felt shits, damns, and stupid assess. But she would never say GD—not one time. For this, I knew I was safe in conquering this new adult underground language.

I would sneak from the front seat of the school bus, slide in with one of the hopeless high schoolers, and go straight for the juggler. "Hahaha, shit, you ain't ever lied." They would pause briefly, probably thinking *what in the hell is this kid talking about*, but then quickly snap back to it because I was one of them, using their language. Most of the time it would be, "Jarrod, you crazy, lol." That's all I needed to feel that acceptance into the community. I had something the other youngsters didn't: street cred.

From there, stealing. Many days, my brothers and I would attend a Boys Club to keep us busy. Mom and Dad really meant to keep me out of trouble, but it only seemed to give me more opportunities to see how the older kids maneuvered through and around trouble.

Nothing Concealed: Veiled Secrecy Will Be Brought To Light

The Boys Club had a cantina, a place to order food, but Mom and Dad would only give us enough for a snack. It was crazy to ask a kid to stay at one place for a couple of hours and not eat, so I took it upon myself with the help of some older kids to improvise.

Getting dropped off at the front doors, I would have to give the "I love you, Mom and Dad." As soon as their rearview mirror could no longer see objects closer than they appeared, I would be on my way up the street. First, I would have to pull my pants down a little lower because the older kids had to see your underwear to let you walk with them, or at least that's what it seemed. Adjusting my pants just right to see my overly worn Hanes, I would start up the hill. Chonci, aka my angel conscience, aka Jiminy Cricket, would always be there. "Jarrod, you better not go and get in trouble. Mom is going to be mad."

"I don't care about her being mad. Damn, she always mad anyways."

Adjusting my pants a little lower because that cuss word earned me a few head nods from the older boys, I quickly turned from Chonci and headed up the street. Chonci, sure, was the first to snitch but was right there with me walking up that hill each time. An old white man owned the store and it had everything: the wax candy that had Kool-Aid inside, Laffy Taffy, chips, Airheads, the hard candies that littered Mamaw's coffee table, sour gum, Baby Ruth, Sugar Babies, and so much more. Before entering the store, we would all huddle up at the fence to get a game plan. Chonci and I had just been gifted some hand-me-down pullover starter jackets, and mine was Orlando Magic, so I was the main culprit. We would all go in at the same time and the older boys would browse the store while I loaded up on as much food as I could in the front pouch of my Orlando Magic starter jacket. Easy enough.

"Jarrod, don't do it."

"Stop being scared, Chonci."

To not be obvious, I would enter the store last, giving the older boys a few seconds head start. We couldn't give ourselves away that soon and alert the owner we were together. Surely, he couldn't remember the same group of kids coming up weekly, bombarding his store, to buy a single item. Surely not. I count to five Mississippi.

"One Mississippi."

"Two Mississippi."

"Three Mississippi." Hell, I can't wait and go rogue. I run in the store, never looking up, stuff as much food into my hand-me-down Orlando Magic Starter jacket, and hit the door runnin'. Of all the times I robbed that store, two things never happened: the food never got low, and the owner never chased me. He would only mumble something loudly that I could never make out. Either way, it was a mad dash down the hill with Chonci in front of me. Chonci was so fast and was always out running even the older kids, so I knew if I was close to him, we would never get caught because that meant we weren't last. We ran to the side of the Boys Club. Exhilarated from the theft, I go into the front jacket pocket.

"Jarrod, you shouldn't have done that," was usually the sentiment Chonci would be scolding me with as he got his share of the Sugar Babies, Atomic Fireballs, wax candy, and whatever else my wide-palmed, small fingers could shove into my jacket. The older kids finally arrived, getting their shares of all the riches I had bestowed upon them. I always seemed to get left with the smallest portion, but who cared because all the laughs and "Man, Jarrod, you crazy" filled me more than any Dum Dum sucker could ever. I don't know how many times we robbed that store, but it was a rite of passage to belong. Cussing and stealing got me nothing but love from the older kids...but fighting sealed the deal for me.

Fights! I was the leader in fights! I would KO a kid before the teachers could even get there to place me at the scene of the crime. I had a set of skills that allowed me to hurt kids quickly then elude and lie. Why tell the truth? I knew the only thing that mattered was making sure it didn't get back to Mom. The teachers wouldn't believe me anyway, so why not sharpen my skills of misdirection and deny, deny, deny, unless there was 150 percent proof I was at the scene of the crime. I became so good at eluding, Mr. Nolen, my elementary school principal, elected me to be the leader of the safety patrol. He was smarter than I thought. He would always come to me if there had been any type of altercation that dealt with being "handsy," as he would always say. Of course, I wasn't a snitch and never told, but for some reason, after my nomination to Safety Patrol, the number of handsy offenses went down exponentially. I told him, "I am just doing my job well and the kids know better than to cross me."

All of these new skill sets spilled over into my friend relationships. I would even antagonize my friends because I didn't know their true motives. Attacking everyone was my number one go-to at all times. If the teacher called my name with the wrong tone, I would lash out. "Watch yo tone." The only, and I mean only, defense my teachers had was, "Jarrod, do you want me to make a call home?" They knew it would buy them a few days, maybe a week before I decide to jump stupid again.

If a kid made fun of me in the bathroom, I would punch first and ask questions later. I was honored to be the only person on the bus to have an assigned seat, the first seat on the bus, behind the bus driver so he could see me in his mirror. I honestly didn't care anymore. A simple, "Is everything okay?" might have set my life on another course. The question was never asked so I went on as though things were normal. I remember my mom crying to me one day asking, "Jarrod, do you just like getting in trouble?" Mom acted as though she hadn't been in the same house that I was with the daily screaming and yelling. Always confused on how you can punish a child for replicating what they see, I understand now that even my mom was becoming apathetic and was in denial of her situation. At some point, I could tell Mom was reaching for change in any direction, which led us to church.

God?

We had always been what I call "Sunday churchgoers." We weren't necessarily involved but my uncle was the pastor of the church, so all Dad's family went, and we had to consistently be a body in the pew as a type of representation. The Sunday morning preparations were no different than any other day of the week: threats, yelling, and tears. The only difference was that we knew we better "act right." Act right meant you had better hold the door for everyone, put a smile on yo face, say yes and no ma'am and sir to any adult that speaks to you, and, most importantly, don't you say anything, I mean anything, that happens between our four walls. On our fifteen-minute drive to church, Kenny G would be playing softly over the radio. I hated jazz, especially Kenny G, but this was Dad's calming anthem and a time for us to get the do and don'ts repeated, just so we knew there were no games being played. There would be silent stares shared throughout the car, but no one dare break the silence. The dreadful harmonizing sounds of the saxophone was the only "churchy" thing happening in the car besides Mom lining the bottom of her purse with peppermints. Mom always seemed to have an extra-large bag of peppermints to unload in her bag on the trip to church. She carried one purse all the time and oh how I loved the remnant smell of peppermints. The peppermint smell would grab hold of you, freezing the hands of time. "Baby, you need a mint?" Without words, I would just nod and stick my hand out. That brief transfer of peppermints from her hand to mine was our way of consoling each other.

    Honestly, I hated everything about church, but especially being dressed up in what Mom and Dad called "Sunday best." Because I knew it was really just oversized hand-me-downs that needed extra tuckings to create an illusion of things being tailored, flea market pointy-toe dress shoes that were doctored up with black shoe polish, clip-on ties, and sample adult cologne from JC Penney. This was all packaged with a "You better be thankful for what you have because most kids don't have this much" speech. I wasn't thankful, and I didn't care what people in the pews thought of me.

I hated the rushed half folded egg sandwich meals and the soggy Capt'n Crunch bowls of cereal in preparation because no matter how early we got up, Dad always made us late. I hated the coffee breath Dad had but tried to cover up with a handful of one thousand Tic-Tacs and mouthwash. Dad would always carry Tic-Tacs and mouthwash with him because he must've known how bad Folgers in your cup made his breath smell. I hated the fifteen-minute ride because I felt like I was holding my breath like everyone did when they drove over a long bridge. The trip was exhausting, trying to playback all the dos and don'ts of my actions with other people. I hated everything about church.

There was nothing to like about church through my eyes except the two women that cooked. My mind always shifted when I entered through the tinted basement door and the aroma of the homemade biscuits wrapped me up like a warm loving blanket. They would always squeeze me so hard and let me sample the food, as if I were special, and would say, "Shhhh, don't tell." Maybe they knew something was wrong or maybe I really was special. Either way, seeing them and smelling the fresh homemade rolls, sweet tea, and pies made me forget about how much I hated church.

As a young child it was some type of honor to be a part of big church. Big church just meant that you would bypass children's church and attend with the adults. I always hated it because they would make you find your parents and sit with them. That was my time to sit downstairs, play, and forget about my life.

My dad was smart in the fact that he would nestle in the furthest back corner pew possible, as though he were doing two things: hiding his sins from the congregation and his brother, Pastor Buddy. I would always place myself on the outside of my mother, sporadically glancing at Dad to make sure he wasn't watching me and to get the slight head nod of approval. I can remember sitting in those old wooden pews listening to my uncle use all the poetic euphemisms, with yells of joy and excitement rumbling through the sanctuary. Sitting there, I wanted to have those exciting yells, but the only thing on my mind was: *who is God and why is he allowing this to happen to us?* How can all these people that talk about hearing from God not hear from him that we are going through so much crap at home? How can my dad and mom drop their heads in prayer with tears in their eyes knowing what just happened a short while ago? It was as if church was a gathering of all the actors and actresses to sharpen and demonstrate their skills they had learned throughout the week. I was angry, sad, and so confused on who this God was.

There are many occasions I remember in the church setting, but in a Southern Baptist "Black" church, Christmas time always stuck out, due to the over-the-top perfume and cologne smells, dresses, hats, suits, and the finest of jewelry being flashed because of God's prosperous favor. How does all this show God's favor on your life, but, hey, if it's good for you. I digress. During Christmas every year we would have to read "stupid" readings in front of the church. I say stupid because they would put simple-minded children in their dress-to-impress attire, in front of the church to recite what they had been half beaten for, so all the adults could googly eye with all their oohhhhs and awwws. I guess, the more laughs and smiles meant you performed even though you stumbled over each word and some random lady with the largest hat in America would coach you, always adding, "You good, baby." We all knew as children this lady got on everyone's nerves because they would almost prepare you for Sister Martha to coach you from the sidelines. We as children were just terrified not to embarrass our parents and family in attendance. We had no idea what we were reciting or even cared. Our validation was from the smiles, head nods, and thumbs up we received during the regurgitation of the words we had been fed over the previous weeks like grass to a cow in the dew of morning. Obviously, Christmas was huge in the church I attended not only for the elaborate costumes, but because this was the time of year the pews were overfilled with new faces of past members and those that are so called "lost." I always played better with the kids that were shunned because their parents were holiday jumpers, which means you show up during holidays, just to let everyone know you are doing just fine, I guess. I prayed to be one of those kids because I imagined their Sunday mornings free of no time constraints, being able to run wild like the little animals we were.

In this season, attending big church was a must because my uncle, the pastor, felt like the children should see how the adults worship and have an opportunity to welcome Christ into their lives.

For the Christmas play, my brothers and I had finally graduated to get true roles and had practiced so hard. I, one of the wise men, stood proud with my staff during what seemed like days of stumbling over words, but we made it. The play was a success, and we got the standing ovation that we had prepared for. Uncle Buddy gave everyone the double-handed stand up gesture and, whether it was earned or forced, we got the standing ovation. Immediately preceding the ovation, we were asked to accompany our parents in pews. We all scattered like ants, some of us soaking in the last of the smiles and laughs by taking our precious time leaving the stage.

It is a monumental time for any pastor because at this time he made an altar call, which means he asked if people needed prayer to come forward. I had asked a few times throughout our big church attendances why Uncle Buddy always ended his speeches with begging.

"Mom, why does Uncle Buddy always beg people to come to the front after he's begged them to put their money in that silver plate?"

"Baby, he just wants people to go to heaven, so he asks a bunch of times in case someone changes their mind."

"Then why do you always tell us to stop begging and asking for stuff?"

"Jarrroooodddd."

I called it the "wear 'em down," technique. I would ask fifteen different ways for something until Mom was like, "Shit! Yes, just get out of my face!" I knew Uncle Buddy would continue to keep asking, always asking, "Is there anyone else?"

I stood with my head down, eyes squeezed tight, trying my hardest not to look up, but I did. Just as I did, Dad and I caught eyes and the look was as if I had better go. There was something that made all the adults in the church yell and praise God harder when they saw the children take that slow walk to the front. I stood a little longer before making that begrudged step to the front of the church. People are clapping and praising God for me walking, but I don't feel anything. I am a child amongst adults, what do you do expect except for me drop my head and follow suit? Once to the front, I nudged myself in between a couple of adults that had come on his first of many pleadings for others to join. And so, it began, the steps a pastor takes the congregation through in order to dedicate your life to Christ.

"This is a huge life-changing moment for you; please repeat after me.

Nothing Concealed: Veiled Secrecy Will Be Brought To Light

"I believe that Jesus was crucified and on the third day he rose again."

"…I believe Jesus was crucified and on the third day he rose again."

He continued, "I know I am a sinner but from this day forth, Jesus has forgiven my sins and I am a new person."

"…I know I am a sinner but this day forth, Jesus has forgiven my sins and I am a new person."

"In the name of the Father, Son, and the Holy Spirit."

"…In the name of the Father, Son, and the Holy Spirit.

"At this time, since you confessed this with your mouth, you are newly saved, the old is gone, and now life has just begun." Shouts erupt in the sanctuary, and when I heard this, my head popped up, started listening, and was truly excited. After church, the excitement continued because the deacons and sisters of the church approached Mom and Dad to compliment them on how great of parents they were for me to dedicate my life to Christ.

Most Sundays, we would rush out the back of the church doors to avoid the nonstop talking. We usually headed to Dad's favorite food place: China House. It was a Chinese restaurant where they knew us by name and always had us a table with three extra plates. This day was different. My life was changed. The only thing I could think was the fights will stop, new home life, no arguing, and no more pain. Everyone is smiling and Dad orders his normal.

"Number 107 please, shrimp in a golden cup." It was a giant fried wonton bowl that was littered with shrimp, carrots, cabbage, mushrooms, and their special sauce that topped it off.

"We'll also have chicken with cashews and extra fried rice." This is the meal that Chonci, Scooter, and Shay would split with Mom. That's why they always had us three plates awaiting us on the table. Dad and I would split number 107 because I always had the largest appetite and didn't waste anything.

The meal is going amazing; Dad is cracking jokes and Mom is talking to people as they pass by. Today was the change we needed, the change Uncle Buddy said would happen. We finish our meal with everyone getting two fortune cookies. They always gave us two fortune cookies a piece as to say, "Thank you." We crunched those down before leaving because Dad didn't like anyone eating in his car. We all loaded in the car and headed home for the best Sunday ever. No sooner than we were pulling into our subdivision, Mom made a comment to Dad, and something triggered him. He forgot about God, church, my dedication, and the China House. He turned his head quickly to Mom and backhanded her in the face. The car went silent, and the remaining five hundred yards to the house took longer than the car ride to church and the whole sermon combined. Mom's hands covering her face, Dad yells, "Kathy, in the room!" We pull up and scramble out Mom's side of the car, trying to avoid a smack. Mom opens the front door to the house, we stumble over each other to get downstairs for comfort, piling up together on the papasan chair. A few minutes of silence and then Mom's room erupts in tears and yelling. You can hear the repeated blows to Mom as she's crying, "Marvin, I'm sorry, stop."

"Don't you ever talk to me like that again!"

We get closer together on the couch and all I can think is, *WRONG, WRONG, and WRONG!* Uncle Buddy lied and God isn't real. He said all things would be new, but it's worse. How can God allow this to happen after I did everything Uncle Buddy told me to do for change? Because of this, my quarrel was no longer with my dad or even the situation I was in but with God.

You can never be outspoken about it in a Southern Baptist "church attending" family but you can harden your heart to any so-called "Good News" the church or anyone else associated with the church is forcing on you. How can God allow these things to take place in our home and not shine light on them when it says all things will come to the light? I wanted my dad to be exposed for who and what he was, but this God wouldn't allow it. I just wanted to be saved from the hurt and pain, but nothing. The Christmas holidays passed by yearly with the same gatherings and benedictions, but life as I knew it was Groundhog Day and the never-ending story. Who was God and why had he bestowed upon me this miserable life? My days in the church became longer, with me becoming more apathetic to the message Uncle Buddy was spewing from the pulpit until that one day…

Seay Holler

Hand out the window making air snakes as the air flows through my arms, listening to the cicadas echo through the holler while Chonci sounds off Lamb Chop's anthem.

> *"This is the song that never ends, yes it goes on and on my friends. Some people started singing it not knowing what it was, and they continued singing it forever just because this is the song that doesn't end…"*

Distracted by the billy goats chewing fence lines while standing atop old, rusted Chevy Novas, cows mooing, and dead deer and possum carcasses littering the edges of the road, while vultures teamed up to devour the stench-stained bodies, until Chonci elbows me to continue. I start in:

> *"This is the song that never ends, yes it goes on and on my friends. Some people started singing it not knowing what it was, and they continued singing it forever just because this is the song that doesn't end…"*

"Y'all better shut all that shit up," but with a snicker and me elbowing Scooter to continue, his small voice started in.

> *"This is the song that never ends, yes it goes on and on my friends. Some people started singing it not knowing what it was, and they continued singing it forever just because this is the song that doesn't end…"*

Scooter could never do wrong because he was the youngest, so I figured in passing the song to him, we would be safe from any lashings. Scooter continued as we snaked through the holler until Dad shut down the song that never ended with "BOYS!" The song came to a halt immediately and we focused back on the journey at hand.

Seay Holler is what Mom called it and where Dad escaped with us just when the mood in the house was like a pressure cooker about to explode. Jeff Seay was one of Dad's longtime friends and he owned ninety-nine acres of country with his house and his parents' right in the smack dab middle.

Jeff was what I saw on the country westerns. He wore a curly greasy mullet, plaid shirts, Justin boots, Wrangler jeans, and carried a hint of stale cigarette smoke on every outfit he wore. He was a gentle soul but was Evel Knievel when it came to any motorized vehicle, especially motorcycles. He would sit on the front handlebars of any size motorcycle, crank the gas, and jump into a wheelie. His mullet would catch the wind like the front tire would and rise. The faster he went the higher his curls and front tire would raise. He could hit cotton pile jumps landing on his back tire and ride figure eights while in that wheelie. He was our personal country western action figure and had a land full of adult toys he let us use however and whenever we wanted.

Along the snake curved roads, random trailer homeowners occupied the holler. The trailers looked as if they were etched into the side of the mountain barely hanging on, with front doors wide open allowing the cool air to circulate throughout the single wide trailers. The trailers would be littered with dirty white people sitting on the front porch doing everything from shucking beans to whittling wood, but all had the aroma of Camels and Newports bellowing through the holler air that would reach the car.

What lay in the cul de sac of Seay Holler was Mr. and Mrs. Seay's single level ranch-style home. It lay bare, built of brown reclaimed farm wood that had one identifying oak tree that disappeared into the clouds. The positioning of the house in the valley with the mountain silhouetting in the background looked like Bob Ross had created it on one of his canvases. To the right of the house was a giant ditch that had the perfect concoction of stagnant water and moisture for breeding grounds of the pterodactyl sized mosquitoes. Immediately south of the breeding grounds stood a cotton pile that only seemed to grow taller with each visit. Directly in front of the cotton pile was a dog kennel that lay barren since I could remember making trips to Seay Holler. A hundred yards from that barren kennel sat Jeff's humble abode. It was a single wide trailer that still sat on four wheels and the slab of cut out mountain. It looked as if Jeff was always prepared to hitch his house up and leave in a hurry.

Jeff wasn't much of a cleaner on the outside of his mobile home, but the inside was spotless. The roof was aluminum with spotty mismatch patch jobs reflecting all the different shades of new to old and rusted metal. The side entrance to his house was littered with beer cans that overflowed multiple trash cans as though he were collecting for one giant lump sum from the recycling company. There was a zero-turn lawn mower sitting in his driveway but never seemed to be used because the grass stood taller than I did. When I say his trailer was spotless, I mean it was naked. He had the bare necessities for mountain living: a television with aluminum wrapped rabbit ears, a blanket that had been torn due to wear and tear that draped over an old beat-up recliner, linoleum checkered white flooring that turned beige due from the mountain dirt, empty cabinets saved for spam and tuna containers, and a fridge that only contained Budweiser—aka "bud heavy" as he would say—and milk. I never saw Jeff drinking around us but whenever I took a glance in his dirty plastic cup, it was always half full of Vitamin D milk.

Once you took the three-to-four adult steps to cover the full square footage of Jeff's house, you would reach the front porch that was littered with a mixture of beer cans and Mad Dog 20/20 bottles. Multiple boards had rotted and fallen, leaving it an unsupported two planked porch. On that two boarded porch, looking across, I would see Jeff's prize possession: the barn. Within the barn were his Evel Knievel toys: dirt bikes, four wheelers, lifted trucks, and anything else that would echo throughout the holler, alarming everyone he was still up to his daredevilish ways. Jeff would add to his collection of drinking cans while he admired all his boy-like toys, dreaming up even more dangerous tricks to accomplish while he pumped himself full of his desired liquids of choice.

Mom would always say, "I can't understand anything he says. It sounds like he's talking with a mouth full of shit." Dad would just chuckle and say, "K-A-T-

H-Y," with her only reply, "WELL." We would all chuckle not knowing what she meant but knew the talk was coming.

Whenever we visited Seay Holler it was a time for Dad to regurgitate how simple life should be and how living like the Seays teaches you self-preservation.

Sitting outside of Mrs. Seay's house by the *Jack and the Bean Stalk* oak tree, Dad would start preparing himself with his speech by clearing his throat. Coughing to get his vocal cords adjusted correctly due to our current change in elevation, "Boys, this is the simple life God wanted us to have. No busy roads, living off the land, and enjoying the peace. This is why, I bring you boys out here, so you can learn how to survive if anything were to happen." I did love Seay Holler but was always confused why Dad didn't mention how horrible the flesh-eating Jurassic Park sized insects were and why he would always hint to the idea of some life altering event happening. I would always speak up, "What's going to happen, Dad?"

"Well, boys, you know Mrs. Seay is preparing for the apocalypse." Before Dad's answer, Mom would do her ghastly exhale and roll her eyes so hard that her pupils would disappear to the back of her head.

"Mrs. Seay says the world is coming to an end in the year 2000 and her pastor is calling it Y2K." Pointing off in the distance, Dad showed us a dirt road that was created by a bulldozer heading to the top of the mountain.

"What is it, Dad?"

"It leads to their bunker." I thought to myself: bunker? Before any of us could ask a question, Dad shushed us because Mrs. Seay came shuffling along waving. Under his breath, "Y'all be respectful and listen." Whispering back in unison, "Yes sir."

By the time Mrs. Seay waddled to the oak tree, Mom had gotten all her eye rolls and heavy breathing out of the way to prepare for the same Alzheimer's apocalyptic talk.

Mrs. Seay was the sweetest lady and was a tight hugger. She was so strong for an old country lady. She would squeeze your neck so hard and chicken peck kiss you on the cheek. "Good to see you babies."

"Good to see you too, Mrs. Seay."

"Y'all, let's go up to the house so I can show you around."

Nothing Concealed: Veiled Secrecy Will Be Brought To Light

I was caught up in watching Mom's continual eye roll and heavy breathing fits. It was obvious she was torn between pretending for the sake of Dad and Mrs. Seay and wanting to scream "you bat shit crazy." She never said anything but just smiled exhibiting those extra-large porcelain teeth.

It must have been a family rule to enter through the side of the house because that was the main entrance of choice for the entire Seay family. Upon entering the side entrance, large wooden spoons and forks hanging from the kitchen wall would greet you with the smell of vinegar from her pickling canned vegetables. Accompanying the large spoons and forks on the wall were one dimensional aluminum roosters and chickens that added to the Seay décor. Mrs. Seay walked around moving her arms like the flight marshallers directing our eyes to the same décor that never moved in our minds but was forever changing and updating in hers. The stove always had pots and pans sitting on it in preparation of throwing together a meal at any moment when company arrived. Mrs. Seay's arms directed us to the living room, passing by the wood paneling that she so loved to show Mom as an updated feature Mr. Seay had upgraded a few years back. The living room was an open space with an old wooden couch that had cushions covered in printed wagon wheels, windows, and flowers. The room was brown on brown, from the couch to the small television with aluminum foil on the rabbit ears. The room was hollow but the aluminum foil on the windows was an eye catcher.

Mrs. Seay scuffled her way to the recliner and plopped down to begin the talk. Dad made a point to make eye contact with each of us, including Mom, to make sure we knew to shut up and listen.

Without delay, "Have y'all gotten your life right with God because soon the world is ending?" Looking directly at Dad, Mrs. Seay said, "Y'all are more than welcome to head up this way to stay here in the holler. We have over ten years worth of food stored up in the mountain and the same amount of water." I puckered up with trepidation in my heart, with inquiring eyes. If Mrs. Seay was so sure that the world was ending, then we needed to get our lives together. And then it began, Mrs. Seay started with what I now knew as the altar call from church.

"Boys, have you accepted Jesus Christ as your Lord and Savior and where is your beautiful sister?" Chonci spoke up immediately, "Yes Ma'am and she don't like camping, so she stayed with her friend Tiffany." I dropped my head to avoid eye contact because I didn't want to tell her the God I knew. It wouldn't have gone over well with any of the adults in that hollow room. Mrs. Seay would look around slightly dazed every few moments and then start back perched up on her recliner, "We have to put this up to protect us," directing our eyes to the aluminum foil strategically placed on the living room windows. Following her fingers pointing to each window, I wanted to ask why but would always get stopped by Dad's piercing eyes, with the "you better not" look. The entire conversation, Mom seemed to be thinking about a grocery list because that's the look she had before we would go shopping. But when Mrs. Seay would scan over to Mom, she would just open mouth smile, and head nod as though she were holding onto every word Mrs. Seay was saying. The conversation would go silent again with Mrs. Seay seeming to get lost in her words and then she would ask, "Y'all hungry?" With that, Mrs. Seay would lose all track of her altar call and shuffle us all back to the kitchen to prepare a meal. Dad would thank her again and Mom would push us out the side door. No food ever got made after those talks but was our formal reintroduction each time we made our way back to Seay Holler.

The fun never truly started until the second day in Seay Holler. "Boys, I told you before, this is the simple life God called us to have. Y'all have to learn how to provide for yourselves in case your mother and I aren't around." I didn't quite know if he and Mom were planning to sneak away and leave us in the dark of night by the way he was talking but I was only focused on getting to the campsite.

The campsite Jeff had thrown together with his bulldozer toy. It lay about a mile north of Mrs. Seay's house and went deep into the woods. You could see that one day, Jeff jumped on his bulldozer and started plowing the ground. He drove it until he was satisfied and cleared out enough trees to plop down his RV. From there, he cleared out more trees to annex the newly renovated dirt with a pond. Jeff said he dug as deep as he could with his bulldozer and then used dynamite to do the rest of the digging. From there, with rain and water runoff from the mountain, a pond was formed. The only other addition Jeff added was the bass and carp to the pond.

The walk to the campsite was long and treacherous for our little feet. The path had obvious trenches from the bucket of the dozer but was slightly smoothed out from all the years of feet pounding it. Jeff wasn't one of perfection,

Nothing Concealed: Veiled Secrecy Will Be Brought To Light

he was more result based and it was to create a place to hide away, and I loved that about him. Larger than life trees canopied over the bulldozed wide path that stretched deep into the woods. About one hundred paces in, the sun became hidden through the trees and the temperature dropped, cooling any record-breaking heat wave. With the shade surrounding on all sides, nature's air conditioning unit turning on, and the light padders of our feet, you could hear the scurrying of animals hidden on both sides of the tree-consumed path. Then all of the sudden, daylight would hit your face, displaying the aftermath of demolition from Jeff's bulldozer. I could always tell when we were getting close to the campsite because of the rope swing.

Before the light hit your face from the shadowed walk, there was a hundred-foot rope that swayed from the wind, alerting us we were at our destination. Jeff must have been intrigued with these never-ending trees like we were, because he climbed as high as his legs would take him and hung a rope out on its single branch that stretched at least fifteen feet. Jeff said he had to hang on the branch and jimmie around on it to make sure it wouldn't fall and once he tied it securely, he shimmied back down the rope. The rope was fifty feet tall and only two or three feet drug the ground.

While the sun still lit up the camp site, the party began. Dad would have us go round up firewood. Jeff had a special mixture of oil and gas to drench the wood in. He said, "Fellas, oil burns slower and hotter, but gas will get the fire started quickly." During the firewood roundup, Mom and Dad would strategically place Jeff's old beat-up military cooler to the side of the RV by their lawn chairs and make it a point to tell us, "Y'all had better not touch this cooler."

With logs on the fire and Jeff saturating them with his special mixture, it was time to light the fire. There always seemed to be a rolled-up newspaper in the RV and Jeff would wind it tight, creating a newspaper wand. He would dip the tip of the newspaper in his special mixture and light it with the tip facing down. The flame jumped on the newspaper and engulfed it immediately. No panic in his bones, Jeff would let the flame climb up that newspaper and right as it was singeing his forearm hairs, he'd toss it on top of the saturated wood. The noise that came off the wood sounded like a giant bubble being popped. The air from that tiny explosion engulfed the wood and the fire was started.

Once the fire was started, Dad started assembling our tent close enough to the fire that it would keep us warm but enough distance away to not melt our cheap polyester Kmart-bought shelter.

Dad would always yell at us to help, "Boys, come help me put this thing together," but it seemed as though he only wanted an audience because he would end up telling us, "Get back out of my way!"

With the fire going and the tent up, the festivities began. Dad, Mom, and Jeff would plop down in those lawn chairs, reach for that old military cooler, and the sound of carbonation being released was the kickoff to our country getaway.

The sun starting to set, crickets sounding off, the frogs bellowing, and the slap fighting with the mosquitos were all precursors to whichever life lesson Dad wanted to teach us on this trip to Seay Holler.

While we chased each other dangerously close to the fire, we awaited the adults to drink their "adult drinks."

"Mom, what is that? Can I have some?" I would ask as Chonci and Scooter chased me around the fire.

"You know you can't have any. Shut up and back up from that damn fire before one of y'all gets burned!"

Jeff was a professional at drinking his milk and adult drinks because while Mom and Dad were sipping theirs, he was working on his third. With a loud burp, we all laugh and go back to dancing with the fire.

We all knew after Dad finished his second "adult drink" he would be ready to give us our life lesson. No sooner than he set the bottle down, he jumped up and said, "Boys, y'all are going to gig tonight."

"Gig?"

"Yes, frog gig. Y'all are going to catch frogs and eat them."

Mom sat up quickly and said, "MARVIN."

"Kathy, if they want to eat, they have to learn how to provide for themselves."

We all looked at each other in disgust but knew we had no choice.

"Boys, go find me some wood that's shaped like a fork."

We had to move quickly because the night was catching us. We searched high and low until Mr. Goodie two shoes, Chonci, found a stick that looked exactly like a fork. He yelled out, "Dad, I found it!"

"Bring it here, son, so I can use my knife to sharpen it."

Dad took that fork shaped stick and began to sharpen the edges with his knife. After a few moments, the tips were razor sharp.

"Here's what you're going to do boys. One of you will hold the flashlight and the other will hold this gig. Once you see the frog, make sure you hold the light in its face and the other will gouge the frog with this gig. You'll have to hold the gig in place until it stops moving."

"Ewww Dad! You want us to kill the frog?"

"Yes, and then skin it to eat."

We all looked at each other with faces of horror but knew we had no choice.

With the dark upon us, Dad said, "It's time boys."

We had worked it out amongst ourselves that I would hold the flashlight, Chonci would do the gigging, and Scooter would stay the hell out of the way.

We made our way to the pond. No sooner than we got to the edge of the fish smelling murky pond, a frog bellowed. I did my job and canvased the pond with my light until we found it. He was looking directly at us. I shined the light in its eyes to blind him and Chonci slowly crept over to it. In my heart, I wanted the frog to jump away but the dumb creature didn't. Chonci got inches away, drew his arm back, and thrust it down as though he were doing the javelin throw. It was a success. He didn't have to hold the gig down, because the force of his throw left the frog lifeless, and blood began to spill out of its body.

I was excited for him, "Yes, Chonci, you got it!" Chonci immediately grabbed the gig as though he were experienced and lifted high to show Dad.

"Good job son. Now you have to skin it."

When Dad said that my body began to shiver. Of course, he selected me to skin it.

"Dad, how do I do that?"

He said, "Figure it out."

We made our way to the light of the fire with the frog's lifeless bleeding body. Sitting down, confused on what to do, I took a deep breath and went for it. I pulled the frog off the gig and used the sharpened points of the gig to cut its legs off. Once I had cut its legs off, I used the gig to make a slice at the fattiest part of the leg. Like a loose piece of thread, the frogs' skin was slightly hanging. I grabbed hold and pulled with all my might. The skin came off with ease revealing veins and pink flesh.

"Dad, I did it. What do I do next?"

"Cook it, son. Find a stick to put the frog leg on and cook it. Make sure you cook it good so you don't get sick."

I shivered again because how was I to know how long to cook a frog leg? And the thought of stabbing a dead frog leg was repulsing. Instead of using a stick, I placed a rock in the fire, let the flames heat it up for a few minutes, and laid the frog leg on there. When it hit the stone, it sizzled but the smell was different than expected.

I yelled, "It smells like chicken, Dad." He laughed in the distance.

Chonci and I politicked who would take the first bite and came to the decision that Scooter should take the first bite since he had done nothing. I picked the frog leg off the stone, handed it to Scooter and, without hesitation, he took the largest bite.

Chonci and I looked at each other in shock but didn't want to alarm Scooter, so we waited a few moments to make sure he didn't pass out or die, and then asked, "How was it?"

Scooter shrugged his little shoulders and said, "It tastes like chicken too," and passed it to me. I passed it to Chonci without taking a bite and he called me a punk, but I didn't care. I needed one more test study to make sure. I waited as Chonci chewed on the frog leg, "It's chewy."

With a smirk on my face, "Is it good?"

"It chewy but tastes kinda like chicken." He handed it to me, and I took one last long examination of the frog leg with the two mouse-like sized bites and took a nibble. After chewing it for what seemed like a few minutes, I swallowed it, and looked at Dad. "It's not that bad and does taste like chicken. Do you want to try Dad?"

"No, there's food for us back at the house."

Mom, Dad, and Jeff finished a few more "adult drinks" and decided to head back to Mrs. Seay's house. Before leaving Dad said, "I want y'all to gig more frogs and learn how to live off the land."

"Dad, why can't you just bring us some food back?"

Nothing Concealed: Veiled Secrecy Will Be Brought To Light

"Son, you have to learn how to provide for yourselves, so you eat what you kill."

Head down in shock, my only reply, "Yes sir."

Mom, Dad, and Jeff disappeared into the night and in that moment, I realized how heavy the darkness was. The dark was so dark that it blanketed the dark. It was so dark that the dark hurt. The dark felt like the heated weighted blanket Mamaw had lying upon her bed, hot and heavy. The stillness with shuttering and echoes of distancing animal cries was horrifying. We could run nowhere and were stranded.

Using the flashlight as our protection, I would shine in any direction that there were sounds. I was continuously moving the flashlight until I came across two things: the old beat-up cooler and a paint can that lay nearby. The focus on that cooler and what Mom called "adult drinks" distracted me from the fear of night. I used the flashlight as my guide to the cooler. Beside it, lay half empty bottles. I picked it up, using the light to make out the letters, and sounded out what the bottle read, "F U Z Z Y N A V E L, P I N A C O L O D A." I had no idea what that was, but with Chonci yelling at me in the darkness, "Don't you touch that or I'm telling," and the curiosity of why they liked drinking these so much, I turned it up. I took two or three large gulps and when that warm foam hit the back of my throat, all the Fuzzy Navel came out of my body through my nose. The burning sensation brought tears that streamed down my face, like when you get punched in the nose. The holler erupted in echoes of laughter that came from Chonci and Scooter. Chonci said, "I told you not to stupid. I bet you learned your lesson."

I had to pick up another Fuzzy Navel and drink it just to prove to him, I didn't care what he said. This time I did learn my lesson, because the warm peach that flowed down my throat, reaching my stomach, instantaneously exploded out of my mouth spraying all over the lawn chairs and that old cooler. Immediately, I found Chonci's eyes with my flashlight and said, "Don't tell Mom or Dad, please."

"Get your butt over here and leave that stuff alone and I won't." On my way to scurry back to the fire, I came back across the paint can and all fear of Chonci telling on me went away again. I casually grabbed it in the shadows and headed back to the fire. Once I got to the fire, Chonci saw I had something in my hand. I used the frog gigging technique, shined the light in his eyes, and heaved the can in the fire. With the light in his eyes, he saw the ambers jump in the air when the can hit the fire.

"Jarrod! What was that?"

"I don't know but you had better back up."

Chonci glanced in the fire and realized it was a paint can. "Why would you do that?"

"I dunno. I just felt like doing it." By that time, the paint can sounded like an angry snake and started to hiss.

"Nothing is going to happen, Chonci. Stop being a punk."

The can began to hiss louder but we had nowhere to go because darkness covered us on all sides besides the campfire and the flashlight.

Suddenly, the can stopped hissing and the only thing you could hear in the woods was the popping and crackling of the wood in the fire.

I looked at Chonci, smirked, and went to shine the flashlight on the paint can in the fire. I began searching for the can and then all the logs exploded off the fire with the loudest BOOM! We all hit the dirt-filled deck and, upon looking up, flame-filled logs were flying everywhere and fire fairies danced in the sky, all throughout the trees.

Then, total darkness consumed us in every direction. "JARROD!" Chonci yells and Scooter starts crying. I was too fearful to cry. I yelled, "GET IN THE TENT!"

We all scrambled to the tent, zipping it closed. We could see the fire fairies still dancing through the polyester tent. It was hot and sweaty in that tent but none of us dared go outside because of the dark. The fire was out and when we hit the deck, I lost the flashlight. We were captives of the night. We all three huddled up in fear of what would happen throughout the night, but none of us ventured to move. Chonci popped his head up, slapped me in the head, and said, "You better hope I don't tell." I knew not to say anything because all I could do was lay there and pray he didn't tell Dad.

We stayed in that three-way fetal position throughout the night, and occasionally I would reach out to touch Chonci and Scooter, making sure they were still there.

Barbershop

Tucked away in the corner of a small shopping center conjoined to a tire shop and sitting perpendicular to Al Williams insurance, the barbershop sat with the door propped open by a broken parking concrete bumper. The half-lit patriotic sign that sat adjacent from the bank was our alert that we were arriving to Ronnie Donelson's Barbershop.

There was always nervous tension in the air when approaching the shop because of the unknown. Dad would always prepare us for what we might see. "Boys make sure to watch what everyone is doing closely but know you don't have to be like them. None of y'all boys came with an owner's manual but if you watch how they all conduct themselves, you can see what not to do. Your capabilities far outweigh your abilities, boys, but it's up to you to not get caught up with the wrong crowd. The people aren't bad that are in the shop but have made bad decisions and because of this, they lost their chances."

By this time, I had stopped listening because I knew what was next. I was just ready to see and hear the nonstop action that awaited me in the shop.

Upon reaching the propped open door, you could see the metal chairs lined with green shiny vinyl along the wall where the next person in line awaited a haircut. Once I stepped inside, the first thing that caught my eye was the speckled tile floor that was no longer white and had faded to a yellowish cream color. Small hair particles floated through the air from the designated sweeper. The designated sweeper was someone who always hung out at the shop, holding a broom, and would randomly jump up to sweep piles of forgotten hair from the ground. Dad said the guy was special, so Ronnie gave him an easy job that he usually messed up.

The first barber chair was occupied by Pete. Pete was quiet, and usually the only communication was a head nod. His words were few and far between but when he spoke it was usually asking how you'd want your hair cut. Pete would occasionally chuckle, showing the gap between his teeth, when Ronnie or someone said a joke where he couldn't fight the laughter back. His eyes were always red and drooping low. Ronnie did most of the talking for him, telling us how many hours he worked at the factory and how he was the only nigga that wanted to come to work after work and that would still work. Ronnie would comment on how Pete was a good old school nigga and a good man.

Pete averaged 1 haircut to Ronnie's 4 to 5 but still had all satisfied customers. Pete was a quiet perfectionist. He would tap you on the shoulder and nod in the mirror to see if you wanted to make any changes. Even though his words were few, we had our own silent language that consisted of head nods and half smirks to let one another know things were copacetic.

The middle chair always stayed vacant but was almost like a dividing line of privacy for Ronnie and Pete. The third lay idle of any haircuts but was used as a recliner for Ronnie, the head barber and owner.

Ronnie had been cutting hair for over forty years and that's why he could talk for what felt like forever but when he actually put the clippers to your head, he would be done in five minutes or less no matter how bad of shape the head he was dealing with. If Ronnie wasn't reclined in his chair, telling jokes, or talking about current issues, he was walking back and forth to the refrigerator. It was an old antique General Electric refrigerator that had a single silver-space-like handle on it and had turned the same beige color the floors had turned due to age and use. Ronnie would two-step back and forth to it, grabbing that space handle and reaching into it for his aluminum foil wrapped secret that was buried deep in the plastic bag from the store's produce department. He always called it his apple. Once he observed his apple and was satisfied, he would reach up top in that GE and grab an ice chilled mason jar. He would take a slight inhale and then exhale of the jar to defog it. It was the kind of canning mason jar because it had the identifying 3D impressions that I recognized from Mom's mason jars.

Once he dug deep into that bag and removed the aluminum wrapped surprise, he would just eye it with delight, kind of mumbling and shaking his head. Right as he was taking a bite, I realized it was not actually an apple but an onion. He took a large delightful bite out of that onion and then drank the clear contents in the mason jar. After he would declare how good it was with a "DAMN," he would wrap the apple back up, shove both the apple and the clear liquid in the old GE, and head back to his leaned position in his barber chair.

Dad liked to get there early to beat the rush but it always seemed to only be a few seats open because there were always unsettled men pacing and talking…talking about sports games, about how much money they won—never how much they lost—how many people were at City Lights and how they were acting. I found out City lights was a nightclub where all the adults went to drink, dance, and what Ronnie called "fornicate."

Pete was the parlay guy. This was one of many reasons he took so long to cut hair. When I got in the chair, I had my mind made up that I was there for the day. No sooner than he made his initial cut, someone would run in to check their numbers. Pete would usually chuckle and take their money. Dang, Pete had the largest wad of money I'd ever seen. I followed his hand as he unfolded the large wad of money that was layered from large bills to smaller bills with all of them facing the same way. Folded in half, I'd see all the hundreds and try to count them as he flipped it open quickly to the center where the dollar bills lay. I'd watch him tuck the money into one of his three barber cape pockets. He'd tuck it away, reach for his paper bag, take a gulp, and refocus on my hair. Pete would lean down and ask the same two questions: "Want a low or high fade? How much you want off top?" I never knew what I actually wanted but would say whatever came to my mouth first and always say, "Take enough off but not too much because I want my waves to show." He would simply nod and go back to work until Ronnie started talking trash.

The police department sat less than 300 yards away but when the police came in to get a haircut nothing changed. The barbershop was like the home base in tag. No one was interrogated or arrested. They would let people gamble, drink, and talk recklessly without any hassling. Ronnie would just look up at the police officer and acknowledge him with a head nod and go back to whatever he wasn't doing. We were all the same.

Every time we were at the shop, there would always be a man that everyone called "Hustle Man" that came by. He wouldn't come all the way in the shop at first but would walk slightly in, waiting for Ronnie to give him the welcoming upward head nod before entering. Upon entering he would go straight into his yelling sales speech. "I got hats,

Fubu shirts, Oakley glasses, VCR's, cameras, and can get you what you need or want!" There would usually be a silencing pause amongst the shop because everyone was computing mentally what Hustle Man had just rambled out and then people would start shouting out, "How much?" Hustle Man was able to keep up by calling out single prices and bulk pricing deals like a cattle auctioneer. He would still be standing by the door and everyone that was littered along the long line of seats would go meet him at the door, exchange money, and I would watch him making multiple runs out of the bell ringing door to grab their merchandise. After he had made all his sales, he would ask, "Is anyone needing anything? I can get what you want or need," and then he would disappear out of the door. Dad never bought anything from Hustle Man but always spoke to him.

The barber shop had no rules other than to be respectful of others and was an open door for "men to be manly men," as Dad would say. No matter where they were in a haircut, if someone jingled change, it was on. Pete would usually be the one to move the woven chairs that sat in the back of the shop perpendicular to the GE to set the stage and bare the beige colored concrete wall that used to be white. Ronnie or Pete would sweep along the wall to make sure nothing would impede the game and raise their arms to allow adequate room for their follow through.

The game was pitching quarters. Grown men with half shaved heads wearing barbers; capes would huddle up while shaking the loose change in their pockets. There was always one that would place their foot on the loot. Before the game started, trash talk was a necessity.

"I'm down a nina."

"Annie up then foo, I'm in a dub."

Everyone one would reach deep down into their pockets grabbing out wads of cash to annie up that nina with a dub. Once bets were safely placed under the holder's foot, the game began. Change jingling in all directions, one half shaved man would squat up and down as though he were trying to warm up his old bones before throwing an underhand pitch. OOOHHHHS and laughs would echo the barbershop while I tried to glance to see where it landed—at least two feet from the wall. "That ain't notin," as the next was up. He had the same technique with the up and down knee bending but he let go of his quarter at the bottom of his knee bend. "OOOHHHHHHHHH, Ok ok, I see ya," floated in the air as his quarter was only a foot from the wall. The last pitcher was up. "Watch how it's done, boys." His technique was completely different than everyone else's. He leaned down as far as he could and flicked his wrist. The quarter hit the ground and bounded all the way to the wall, leaning up against it. With a laugh, "Pay up foos!"

With the money firmly under the foot holder's foot, Ronnie proclaimed, "House always gets his 10%." They would pitch quarters until someone got mad because they gambled too much money away and then Ronnie would calm the shop down by reaching in the fridge for his apple and shine, heading back to his designated spot at barber chair 3. Once he got back to the chair, everyone else would assume their normal seated position in line and go right into talking about the sporting games the night before.

We would all be done with our haircuts and you could tell Dad felt obligated to stay around a little while longer to talk with Ronnie, and then after he mentally wrestled with the fact of sitting any longer in the shop Dad would proclaim, "It's always great to see you, Ronnie." Dad would dig back into his pocket and secret handshake Ronnie and Pete with a tip.

Once in the car, Dad would start back up with his speech, "No matter what you see in the shop, it stays in the shop boys. Do you understand me?"

In unison, "Yes sir."

"There are things you hear and see in that shop but you don't ever do or repeat."

"Yes sir."

Even though I agreed with my "yes sir," I loved the energy and atmosphere of the barber shop. I loved the trash talk, gambling, lies, and everything that came along with our $10 haircut. As a child, I felt at home in the barbershop and could tell those men thought like me.

Cuz

"He's not house trained and is bad for the kids to be around Kathy," Dad would say while Mom blankly stared off in the distance, not hearing a single word. Dad never liked my cousin coming down to our house...but how could Mom deny her nephew time with his cousins?

"Kathy, a damn juvenile delinquent doesn't need to be down here with the boys."

"He's my nephew and it'll do him good to get out of Morristown, Marvin."

While Dad usually got his way, these arguments always seemed to sway in favor of Mom.

The sporadic nights he would stay with us gave us the idea that our Aunt just needed a "damn quick break." He wasn't a bad kid — he just did what he wanted to do and didn't care about the consequences. When he came around, all of us shadowed his every movement, awaiting the moment he would propose his exhilarating sneaky mission impossible ideas. But he didn't last long at our house. He was like a forty-eight-hour stomach virus, because after he had run his course, it was time for him to go home.

The weekend with my cousin started out normally. We were doing the usual: rough housing, trash, and picking fights with the neighbors.

I had a fascination with rocks—and throwing them. It always ended up with someone's body part running into my rock, nonstop tears, and me getting whipped. But the fascination never died. Our driveway was nothing but gravel, so they begged me to pick them up and try all the arm angle reckless throws until the inevitable screams and tears.

I stood in the driveway sort of scuffing my feet along the top of the gravel until I ran across a beautifully made throwing rock. It was long and slender and the perfect lake skipping rock, so I had to pick it up. Tossing it back and forth glancing at the rock, my brothers, cousin, and neighbors, I had an amazing lightbulb idea: rock throwing war.

"Chonci, let's get teams and have a war."

"Jarrod, you know better."

Tossing the rock back and forth from hand to hand must have hypnotized mister goodie two shoes, because before you knew it, "Scooter is on my team."

"I got cuz." After that we knew the weak links were the neighbors, so we divided them evenly. All of them on Chonci's team.

It is World War II, running, hiding, screaming, shrapnel flying everywhere, until teams take cover in their trenches, two huge sea green junipers that were a few years due for a trim.

Stocked up on ammo and tucked away in our bunkers, war is unleashed.

Erratic arm angle throws, screams and laughter erupt, from raining down on juniper and destroying their base.

"STOP, Jarrod, you hit me in the head!"

"HAHAHAHAHAHAH, YESSSSS!

"STOP crying, punks."

A few more missiles are dropped and tears ensue.

"OUCH!"

Mom hears the pleas of defeat and busts out the back screen door.

"Jarrod, what the hell are y'all doing?"

"Nothin, Momma, nothin."

"Then why do I hear tears?"

Maurice was our best friend that lived up the street and was always made to jump in any game to even the numbers. But of course, Maurice ends up hurt again.

"EVERYBODY AND I MEAN EVERYBODY, GET Y'ALL BLACK ASS IN THIS HOUSE!"

As we were coming into the house, Mom was waiting by the door to make sure to slap me upside my head.

"Didn't I just tell you about those damn rocks?" SMACK

Even though the war was over, we still had Super Nintendo, so it wasn't that bad of a punishment. Plus, we only had to stay quiet for a few minutes for Mom to forget about us — out of sight, out of mind. After wrestling, playing Nintendo, and dirtying up the house like any other day, it was time for bed.

"I got the top bunk," my cousin said before anyone else could claim it. Chonci just looked at me, so I knew what that meant: floor pallet.

We had these heavy wooden bunk beds that Dad had gotten for a great steal price at the flea market. The shredded bottom of the wooden box spring was cardboard patched and what I stared at most my nights from my bottom bunk position.

You were the king of the room if you had the top bunk position. I was always traded back and forth between rooms, so I was never in the running to hold the king of the room position and whenever someone stayed the night, which was often, I would still end up on the bottom bunk or the floor somehow.

The floor pallet wasn't as bad as it seemed. Mom would take a bunch of smelly old comforters that sat in our old chest downstairs and stack them like she was making a fluffy cake. Old smelly comforter on top of old smelly comforter until she stood back and looked in satisfaction. Even though the covers were stacked high, as soon as I plopped down, I felt nothing but floor. Still, it was satisfying to know I had an unlimited roll around sleep range. Whatever the covers touched was my domain.

We laid there laughing for what seemed like forever. No jokes but empty glances around the room catching each other's eyes, inciting a laughter riot.

"Cut all that damn snickering out and go to bed!"

This just caused us to laugh harder for no reason.

"Don't make me come in there. Shut it up!"

These were all idle threats that would add flames to our laughter until Mom would jostle things around as though she were getting up.

That's when we knew the snickering had gone too far and would just lay there sporadically laughing until we were fast asleep.

I'm a light sleeper and could wake up at any moment from erratic movements. My cousin was tossing and turning on the top bunk making a lot of noise. It didn't startle me but caused me to start my sheep counting back over.

Lying on my stomach on the king size floor pallet Mom designed for me, I feel my cousin tap on my shoulder. Kind of groggy, "Cuz," but not too loud because Mom would definitely come in there.

Slightly nudging me as if he were trying to wrestle, I shrugged away.

Shrugging away did nothing. He grabbed my wrist. I pulled away. He pressed his swollen outside smelling body against my back.

His head nestled near my ear with heavy sloppy breathing, "Be quiet, Jarrod."

I was frozen, paralyzed by shock and fear.

Not knowing what to do, I did nothing.

I didn't know what to do.

Terrified, smushed between the king size floor pallet and a sloppy swollen teenager, I pressed my face deeper in the floor pallet wanting it all to go away.

With my eyes deep in the covers, I can hear his asthmatic heavy breathing.

He slides his hand to the top of my Hanes and aggressively pulls them down. I dig deeper into the pallet squinching my eyes even tighter.

I cross my legs and try to crawl away, but his sloppy swollen body holds me pinned.

He starts to breathe heavier and I squeeze my legs tighter.

He leans all his weight on my upper back.

I can't breathe.

The only thing I can think about is breathing.

I exhale and feel a painful pressure.

He begins to shove his weight forward and the pressure starts to increase. It felt like right before a balloon is popped.

Tensing my entire body, especially my legs together, I feel a pop. The most excruciating pain ran from the bottom of my feet to the top of my head.

Oh, how I wanted to scream, but the pain was so intense it took my breath and all emotions away.

He began shifting his sloppy swollenness back and forth, back and forth until he just stopped.

He took a deep breath and used my back to hoist himself off me. All his weight in the middle of my back took the rest of me.

Lying there numb, I inhale deep with my Hanes down and pull the covers over my head.

Heavily breathing, sounding like King Kong, he makes his way back atop the bunk, while I lay terrified in the pitch black.

Nothing Concealed: Veiled Secrecy Will Be Brought To Light

Terrified he would come back down later in the night, I stayed awake, covers pulled high but knowing I could do nothing but scream this time.

The night turned to early morning and nothing happened.

In the morning, everyone prepared for their day as normal. Mom made her ritualistic weekend morning gravy-n-biscuits, and everyone moved about loudly and noisily as you can imagine with eight or nine people in a small house.

My mind was a typhoon of emotions.

Do I say something?

Do I cry?

Do I scream?

Do I raise hell?

Do I run away?

I did nothing.

I went along with the day as though nothing happened while dying piece by piece inside.

When he looked at me that morning, he acted as if nothing happened. I watched his every move to see if he was thinking about it the way I was. The only thing he could think about was smothering his plate with the third and fourth servings of biscuits and gravy.

How could they not know something was wrong? How could he eat all those biscuits covered in gravy knowing what he had done the night before?

The morning festivities continued with more eating and people talking over one another, but I was lost within myself.

Confused as to what to do or say, I said nothing. I ate side by side with my cousin, lost in all emotions.

Later that morning, his time was up, so my Aunt pulled up, blew the horn, and he went waddling out the door.

He left but my feelings hadn't.

Was gay now?

I didn't stop him and said nothing.

If what my uncle had said was true, I had just signed my waiver directly to hell. I knew I might be safe if no one ever found out.

At that moment, I internally declared a lifetime of silence.

Sex

At this point in my life, we are always a part of big church now. Sitting with Mom and Dad in the far corner pew, shaking our heads in random agreement with Uncle Buddy, and now carrying a Bible that got us many comments from the other adults, "We are so proud of you and the example you are for all the other kids." These words of encouragement were usually toward Chonci. He enjoyed it when the adults saw him as the "good" child. The other adults would usually just give me a pat on the head and a quick smile because they knew I was bad and owned every bit of it. Even though I was numb to the teachings, I heard every one of them. Maybe, it was the charismatic approach Uncle Buddy would take in his deliverance. I could tell when he was about to press in on a message. He would slightly bend over, squint his eyes, place one hand on his back, squeeze that perfectly folded handkerchief, and start shuffling his feet to the rhythm of the choir. The sanctuary would follow suit. Everyone would sit on the edge of their seat in anticipation for what was next. He would wipe his face with the handkerchief, stand up tall and let everyone have it. "I can do all things through Christ which strengthens me," he would quote from 1 Philippians 4:13. The sanctuary would erupt in tears and screams of joy. Just when he knew he had them, he would go right back into his ritualistic deliverable approach. It would only seem to excite the sanctuary even more. Dang, Uncle Buddy was a great hype man playing to the crowd. I would accidentally remember these scriptures due to memorizing his preemptive approach before driving home his point. I was the copycat champ in practicing his delivery on my brothers and sister. Bent over, one hand on my back, aggressively pointing if I finally caught them doing something wrong.

"Chonci, thou shalt not lie, you damn liar," when he would blame me for eating the last moon pie when Mom told us, "We bet not eat shit before dinner!"

"Jarrod, get over here!"

"I told you I didn't do it Mom."

"Shut your ass up and get over here." I would walk over to get the anticipated slap across the back of my head that would wrap around to the side of my face leaving the imprint of her middle and pointer finger as a reminder of the lies. "You better not cry, or I'll give you something to cry about."

"Yes Ma'am."

"Chonci, smirking in the distance, enjoying me getting punished for his sin.

Shay's sin would be that of modestly dressing—or lack thereof. Shay would do what I call the quick switch every day on the bus. "My daughter will not walk around here looking like a whore," Dad would say, talking to Mom but loud enough for Shay to hear. Dad didn't allow her to wear makeup or revealing clothes.

Shay was masterful at the quick switch. Only one bathroom and six people getting ready, she would use our own time constraints for her sleight of hand magic tricks daily. While we were getting ready, Shay would load layers of clothes on top of clothes. No one ever noticed because we were all scrambling to get ready, balancing the three or four half folded microwaved egg sandwiches Mom would push on us, and not miss the bus. With her face bare and being covered head to toe like *Little House on the Prairie*, we would make our way to the bus. I, taking my number one position on the bus behind Sam, got to see everyone else on my bus stop get on. Upon entering the bus, Shay would be the cute, homely girl. As soon as Sam reached for the long lever to close the folding doors, Shay would begin her transition. Looking up in the driver mirror, I could see her tearing and stripping away clothes. We would both glance at each other briefly in the mirror, but she would win the intimidation stare down and I would drop my head within seconds. I would glance up sporadically, catching her holding that little circle mirror in her hand fully extended as she patted her face with foundation. She would always wait until right before the bus entered Jefferson Middle School before applying the ultra-red lipstick and smushing her lips together on a piece of notebook paper. I didn't know what the notebook paper was for, but I knew when I saw her make this calculated movement, the ride was coming to an end. Being elected first seat rider, I had another privilege that most didn't realize—I had to wait until the last person exited the bus before I could.

Nothing Concealed: Veiled Secrecy Will Be Brought To Light

This was the best part about my celebrated position. I could talk and mess with everyone as they exited to get my day started off on the right foot. Shay would always let everyone go before her just so she could make the final adjustments to her makeup and clothes. Waiting a few minutes for everyone to clear out, she would make her way off the bus as if she were on a runway. As she took the slow walk down the aisle, looking me in the eyes, "Keep you damn mouth closed Jarrod, you hear me?" On the days I thought I was tough, "Don't be no whore, Shay." She would flinch, give me a few swift slaps to the back of the head that seemed to go invisible to Sam, and keep her Tyra Banks runway walk going. Observing her full transformation, she would have a full mask on: eyeliner, blush, ultra-red lipstick, and eyeshadow. She would also have the most up-to-date Brittney Spears skimpy schoolgirl outfit on with the old rag-o-muffin clothes stuffed away deep in her bag.

"Shay, you better stop lying and don't be no whore."

These practiced deliveries Uncle Buddy did never seemed to be the antidotes for me and always led to unwanted fist and kicks of fury.

It was a normal Sunday, and we were attending big church, but things would soon change. Uncle Buddy was deep in a message and then things seemed to take a different turn; the sanctuary became very restless and unsettled. Uncle Buddy was obviously saying something that made everyone uncomfortable, so I dug into my seat and started listening. He began to talk about adultery and homosexuality. Still unsettled, people were looking around which made me perk up and slide to the edge of my seat even more. To see adults at the end of their seats in a squirmish manner aroused my attention even more because it was obvious he was talking directly to them. Back and forth with my eyes, on Uncle Buddy, then the congregation, and then back to Uncle Buddy, he went deep into the topic of adultery.

"If you are married, and your eyes wonder, then you have committed adultery with your eyes and should repent. If you are (the word that stuck with me) philandering with someone outside of your marriage, then you are an adulator." It was a total silence upon the sanctuary, but many women all over the sanctuary exchanged side-eyed glances. But this didn't faze my uncle because he was a fire and brimstone type of pastor that did not hold back even when there was a distasteful flavor in the air. The silence only seemed to light a larger fire under him, as if it were added gasoline to his fire of conviction over the sanctuary. There were no shouts or cries of joy but only side eyes and sighs from the crowd. I was confused because the conviction he spoke with I actually caught and felt. It carried on for what felt like hours and then it happened: the fiery condemning speech of homosexuality. It was a word I didn't know but the tone shifted from the adultery lashing he gave to a tone of "if you even think about this type of sin there is a deeper darker hell that awaits you." I can and never will understand why pastors weigh sins, but I knew when he spoke of this sin it must have been at the top of his list. He stood at his podium for a moment looking around, kind of leaning into the congregation to grab everyone's attention even more. He slowly looked and began to talk about how confusion caused men to lay with men in a sexual manner. I never remember him talking about women but emphasizing how it was detestable for men to lay with other men.

At that moment, I became terrified because I realized everything that had happened with my cousin was wrong, but I had done nothing to stop him. Am I going to hell because I didn't stop it? As Uncle Buddy went more in-depth, "Committing these lascivious acts are condemning you to a lifetime of fire and gnashing of teeth!" Slowly looking over the crowd, Uncle Buddy looked at me. Consumed by cold chills and digging my fingers deeper into the clothe wood pew, I became horrified in wondering if God knew what I had allowed. Am I going to hell? I have to be going to hell! As Uncle Buddy continued, "Christians do not act in this manner towards one another, and God will turn his face from you." My thoughts were swirling with confusion, fear, and anxiety with the thought, "Am I?"

Am I?

Am I gay? After the moments of my uncle talking about homosexuality, it opened the daily mental tug-of-war: doubt, denial and secretiveness. I knew Uncle Buddy talked about men sexing other women that weren't their wives and men sexing other men but what about old women and children? The gripping reality was that I knew it was wrong but I never stopped it. How can I tell Mom, Dad, teachers, or even friends that I was going to hell because I was gay? Even though it felt wrong with the Lady, it was a woman and God can forgive me for that, but a man touching me is the worst wrong possible, Uncle Buddy said. I would tell myself so often, "Jarrod, just don't think about it and it'll go away." I couldn't shake the thoughts. In class, outside at recess, in the shower, and with my friends, the fear of God hating me because I was gay haunted me. How could I let this happen and not say anything? If Mom and Dad find out, they'll disown me.

Now, sitting in the pews at Bethel Baptist Church, I was locked into a gripping roller coaster ride wondering what would happen to me next because I was a gay sinner. Every sermon now, Uncle Buddy was talking to me and the only thing I took from it was, "Jarrod, you're going to hell for what you have done!"

Days, weeks, months, and years after this sermon, all I doubted was my sexuality. No, I was never attracted to a boy or man but if what my uncle was saying was true? Then I am going to the deepest darkest place in hell.

Rough housing with my brothers, I go to grab Chonci around the waist to pick him up and slam him. Chonci was the smallest of the three boys, and I was the largest, so it always made me feel like the king of the mountain to pick him up and slam him. "You gay, get out from behind me faggot!" Hurt but covering it up with anger, I slam him to the ground. He laughs, "You gay and soft." All out war ensues. We fight like we don't know each other until Mom opens the door and screams, "Y'all cut out all that damn noise, and if somebody gets hurt, I'm bustin everybody ass!" Not knowing what Mom would do, we stop but he looks at me, "You a pussy and gay." Is there something wrong with me?

Fighting so many more thoughts in my head, the only thing to do was grab hold of silence. If I tell no one then they'll never know I am gay or that this even happened. The silence became my communication. Everywhere I turned, there was an opportunity to out me as the gay I was.

Growing up poor, there were many ways my parents would try to pinch pennies. One of those ways was to make us three boys bathe together. I hated this more than anything. As soon as we heard the bath water running, we would all debate to take a big boy shower. "Mom, I can hurry and take a shower by myself, I'll turn the water off, lather, and then rise off."

"Shut up and get your ass in this bath." For some reason, my spot usually ended up in the middle, Chonci on one side, and Scooter usually getting near the faucet because he would whine until we just gave in. I would take my clothes off so quickly and hop in the tub trying not to make eye contact with anyone. If there were a stare that lasted a millisecond too long, "Stop staring you fag."

"Shut up Chonci, you're a punk."

"You're the one looking at me queer."

Mom annoyed, "Both of y'all shut the hell up before I get my switch on y'all naked asses."

Surely, my brothers and sister didn't think I was gay as well? Am I gay?

The times we were able to shower by ourselves, I would not even want to. Mid-lather, I would get nauseous and just let the water run over me. It felt like a million bugs under my skin. The way the soap ran down between my back felt like those hands gently caressing me and made me clench my butt cheeks tight. The way I cleaned myself around my private area with the soapy washcloth made me wince and feel as though someone else were massaging my pee-pee. I would still be paralyzed in disgust and fear if it wasn't for Mom yelling, "Stop running out all the damn hot water, and get your ass out!" Mom would say, "Jarrod, you stink," but she didn't know many times I would lock myself in the bathroom, sit on the toilet, and just let the shower run to avoid that feeling from touching myself in the shower. I would at least stick my head in the shower because I knew if Mom didn't see my hair wet that would be two whoopins: one for

Nothing Concealed: Veiled Secrecy Will Be Brought To Light

wasting water and another for not taking a shower because as she would say, "You smell like outside."

To have a world unlocked for you at such a young age is dangerous, especially when the world is you running from an all-consuming shadow. No one to talk to—not adults, family, or friends—leaving only destruction and isolation. Mom explained it to other parents as "Jarrod is a loner," and "he has a quick temper." Isolation at such a young age fighting the demonic thoughts of your own mind is like being locked in the psych ward of your own mental asylum with the straight jacket tied so tight you can't breathe, and it wrapped up around your mouth only letting you see what's happening but not being able to speak about it. Each interaction causes the mental walls of the asylum to close in and that jacket to become tighter and tighter. The straw that broke the camel's back was soon to come.

5-5-5 Video

Whenever Dad blamed Mom for the outstanding late and rewind fees at Blockbuster, Mom would dig down deep into her purse that was larger than Santa Clause's satchel to grab the next option: a movie from 5-5-5 Video. I would sigh because this place just wasn't the same.

The building sat perpendicular from the Family Dollar store, neighbored a floral shop that had a beautiful marquee arrangement but lived with the closed sign swaying in the door, and other hollowed out spots that were littered with the remnants of failed business ventures. Mom called it a strip mall.

5-5-5 Video was bland like unseasoned food. It wore a stale smell and had strategically placed buckets to catch the water falling from the ceiling. The carpets had stains on them that looked like giant black eyes. The trailer park that sat behind the strip mall housed a community of white people with no teeth that walked around like zombies. I would always get caught staring with amazement on how these zombies floated along throughout the strip mall. With a slap in the back of the head, "Jarrod, stop staring."

"What's wrong with them people Mom?"

"They didn't go to school and hung out with the wrong people."

"But why are they walking around like dead people?"

Irritated with my questions, "Drugs Jarrod, it's drugs. Don't do drugs or you'll end up like they druggy asses."

Unlike Blockbuster, 5-5-5 Video had all their movies on the shelves, accompanied with their boxes, almost enticing the zombies to wander in for a higher foot traffic count. There were no special signs illuminating new releases. It was just hand cut poster board arrows taped against the walls. Old movie posters lay jumbled at the checkout trying to arouse any impulse buyer.

Chuck, the owner of 5-5-5 Video, and his wife were the only workers, who, with the ding-dong of our entry through the front door, would welcome Mom by name, "Hello Kathy." Dad never accompanied us to 5-5-5 Video, but Chuck always asked about him and Mom. With her shifty lying eyes, Mom would never give Dad's true whereabouts.

"How is Marvin doing?"

"He's doing great but doing yard work again."

In my mind, I couldn't remember the last time I saw Dad doing yard work because he had us doing everything. Looking at Mom cockeyed just to let her know I was onto her lies, she would just bite down on her jaw and smile, alerting me to pick something and shut the hell up.

Mom usually gave us two movie choices: one for the boys and one for Shay. Mom always let her get movies PG-13 or higher but if I even looked down those sections, I would get the stare of death. After we had rummaged through the old beat-up boxes and stirred up the moldy smell in the carpet with our feet, Mom would threaten us to hurry and choose a movie. It would take more than the allotted few minutes because the majority didn't rule in our ballot casting. Scooter was just there to agree with both parties, so there was never a tie breaker between Chonci and me. Chonci would always use his seniority with, "I'm the oldest, so I get to choose," and I would just disagree because of his overly used stance. With Mom giving the "you better hurry y'all asses up and choose or there won't be any movies" look, Chonci would get his way and choose his movie. We were always curious what Shay was choosing but she was in the especially moldy VIP section that read "18 or older, unless accompanied with an adult."

Upon checking out, Chuck's normal routine was to remind Mom of our outstanding balance but always follow up with, "I'll take care of it this time but don't forget to rewind," and with Mom's lies again, "Thank you and I'll make sure to get them back on time."

Once home, Mom made us go upstairs to watch our movie and informed us, "Y'all better leave your sister alone downstairs because I don't want to hear it. Do you understand me?"

The only acceptable response was, "Yes Ma'am."

Nothing Concealed: Veiled Secrecy Will Be Brought To Light

Popcorn made and movie on, all three of us lay upstairs on the floor watching Chonci's movie. It wasn't that bad, but I couldn't let him know it was a good choice, so I lay there stoic. During the movie, the only thing I could think about was what Shay watching. I decided to wait until the coast was clear and sneak downstairs.

It only took a few moments for Chonci to yelp out loud with his annoying laugh and I knew my chance had come. I inched my way to the basement door and made my move down the stairs. The basement was in total darkness, except the smaller television that was sitting atop the old wooden floor model. I edged myself to the corner of the papasan chair so I could get a glimpse while still hidden enough by shadows to be overlooked by Shay.

On the TV, there was a group of people dancing around like drunken flamingos, staggering around taking turns sticking their heads into what looked like dark paint. I gave myself up immediately in those hidden shadows, "SHAY, what are they doing?"

Strangely unbothered I was there, she laughed and said, "They're eating someone's heart!"

Immediately, I went to playing every infant's favorite game of peekaboo but frozen stiff with fear. All I could do was peep through the cracks in my fingers. The people on the video were all taking turns eating a heart, spreading the blood all over themselves, and dancing. I began to cry, "Shay please turn this!"

"Shut up! Your lil ass came down here tryin to be grown, so you're gonna watch it now!"

She grabbed me, placed me in front of the TV, and wrapped her legs around me like she was playing a game of twister. I couldn't move. She grabbed my hands, holding them so I couldn't hide behind them. She made me watch them dance around in blood, screaming joyfully, throwing their hands in the air to celebrate.

I finally fought free and hid back behind my hands. "TURN IT SHAY, PLEASE."

"You a pussy, Jarrod! Ok, ok I'll turn."

I knew I could come out from behind my palms because the loud click of the VHS player alerted me the scene was being fast forwarded. I still stayed slightly hidden behind my only protection. It hummed for a few moments before she said, "You can open your eyes, punk."

Taking my hands down I realized this scene wasn't so bad. It was a group of 4 or 5 people sitting at a table. The table stood out because it had a small circle opening in the dead center of the table. The people were sitting around talking in a different language and the waiter brought a monkey out for their table.

At first, everyone was admiring the monkey, passing it around, letting it run up their arms and sit on their shoulders. Then a hush came over the people at the table. The man handed back the monkey to the waiter.

"What are they going to do Shay?"

I could feel her legs start to recoil around my legs even tighter.

"Shut up and watch. You'll see." The waiter moved the table apart and began to place the monkey's neck in the hole. The monkey started kicking and making its wild calls, to no avail. The waiter closed the table shut and the monkey's head was atop the table with squirming hands and feet below. Looking at everyone, the waiter gave a head-nod to the gentleman closest to him. Sitting on the edge of my seat, "Shay, what are they going to do?"

"Shut the hell up and watch." The waiter pulled a small meat tenderizer out of one of his pockets, leaned over the table, and gave a fast swing. CRACK! The monkey started frolicking. I tried to cover my eyes. She beat me to it by capturing my fingers, "You wanted to watch my movie, so you're going to watch!" I tried to fight to keep my hands over my eyes, but she was too strong. She wrapped her legs over mine even tighter, holding my hands and feet still.

With another swift strike, CRACK! Blood began oozing and the monkey went limp. I was in shock, just staring at this lifeless body while Shay draped over me. The waiter handed everyone at the table a spoon. "No Shay, please don't make me!"

"Shut up and watch!" The first guy shoveled the skull out of the way and took a bloody spoon full of brain. Looking at everyone, he took a bite. With a cheer, everyone dug in for their share of bloody monkey brain until there was nothing but flattened flesh lying on the table.

I tried to fight her off again but had nothing left. I sat lifeless just like the monkey on the table. I tried to cry but nothing came out. I tried to scream but nothing came out.

Nothing Concealed: Veiled Secrecy Will Be Brought To Light

Shay uncoiled herself from around me, shoving me away, chuckling as she asked me, "You like your first Faces of Death movie? Next time you won't bother me when I'm watching my movie."

"Why do you like stuff like this, Shay?"

Apathy and bewilderment covered her face but with a shrug, "I dunno. I just do," had to suffice.

Terrified that I might've interrogated too much, I just sat in the mugginess of the basement with my head hung low.

"Stop being so scared, Jarrod! Yes, it's real but that's life."

"It doesn't have to be, Shay."

"Well, it is! You better not tell Mom you watched this. If you do, you'll end up like that monkey! Do you understand me?"

"Shut up, Shay!"

With a shove and jab cross combination, I shook my head in agreement to avoid anymore of her terroristic attacks.

I disappeared back into the shadows, but my mind began to flutter back and forth with so many questions. Why did Mom allow her to rent this movie? Why did she laugh and enjoy watching this scary evilness? How was I going to sleep knowing there are people out there that eat human hearts and monkey brains? Was Shay going to hurt me like that monkey?

I had only one option and that was silence. Again.

The Hulk

Pants ripped, mutated green skin, bulging glassy eyes, and the inflation of muscles during a fit rage was what I loved about the Incredible Hulk. Watching the Hulk depower his enemies was invigorating. I would scream at the TV while on the edge of my seat, "DESTROY HULK, DESTROY!" I even prized how he humbled his own Avenger legion. Even the other superheroes couldn't control him during his fits of rage. This was endearing to me. I knew every episode would lead to the Hulk transforming into the green hand smashing ball of destruction and each time I would scream and yell, "YES," telling myself mentally, "I wish I was the Hulk," and thinking about what I would do if I had those powers.

Oh, how I revered the Hulk and his never backing down attitude. But as much as I revered the Hulk, I also feared him because of the way he crept into my dreams like a cunning burglar. I would wake up in pools of sweat with my blanket as my only line of defense. Sweating and curled up in a fetal position, my blanket pulled over my head was the forcefield needed to get back to sleep. Even though night terrors of the Hulk destroying me began to consume me, I still couldn't seem to shake the complete awe I had for him.

One Saturday morning Dad came downstairs in an early fit of rage. He and Mom started early this morning fighting, but it didn't stop me from watching another episode of the Hulk. My eyes were glued to the television when Dad came walking up behind me. I'm half listening to him scream about getting ready for some yard work and all the sudden I'm levitating off the ground. I snapped back to reality and Dad had me grabbed by my arm and was hitting me. "DON'T YOU EVER IGNORE ME WHEN I AM TALKING TO YOU!" The flood gates released and my face instantly became drowned in my tears. "Yes sir."

"Now get your ass up and let's get ready to work."

"Yes sir."

Completely dazed about what just happened, I started scrambling while catching the last moments of the Hulk destroy the city out of the corner of my eyes.

"Do you hear me son?!"

"Yes sir!" I about face, and in that moment, I saw Dad's luminous eyes, the protruding cheek muscle from his clenched jaw, and his muscles popping out everywhere.

Dad was the Hulk. Dad was the superhero that visited me in my nightmares and that I saw daily.

Dad was full of destruction, but everyone on all sides of our lives loved him.

All Dad knew was to create fear and destruction.

Gifted athletically, he was a top world ranked golden glove boxer and a fourth-degree black belt martial artist.

Dad was the Hulk.

Dad was Dr. Bruce Banner.

Dr. Bruce Banner was the alter ego of the Hulk. Like Dr. Banner, Dad was very calculated in everything he did. To the outsiders, Dad was the softest, most kindhearted soul, but I knew the monster inside was always lurking in the shadows ready to destroy. Unlike Dr. Banner, Dad could control his emotions outside the four walls of the Houston jail and, like Dr. Banner, Dad's struggle was himself.

The same green rage I admired on the television, I feared with Dad.

Dad received his powers from his father and the early death of his mother.

Dad's father was an angry dead-beat dad that abused his mother until he was one day gone, out of his life.

His mother's death caused him a lot of pain. When Dad talked of her, there was confusion in his voice. He would talk about how strong she was in raising six children and how she loved so hard, all for it to be lost to cancer.

On our father-son sidekick weekends, he would tell me these things with large water droplets collected in his eyes, but in a moment evaporating as he refocused back in on his silence.

Dad would talk to me as though I were his best friend, telling me all his deepest darkest struggles, from his father to bills not being paid.

"Son, I never had a father around, so I am doing the best I can." I would just sit in silence as his hand gripped my thigh tighter from the driver seat.

Nothing Concealed: Veiled Secrecy Will Be Brought To Light

I was there to listen and, in those times, I loved the Hulk inside of Dad as much as I did Dr. Banner.

Dad was more than just Dr. Banner and the Hulk.

He had multiple personalities, but you never knew which one would be assigned until a situation was presented.

My favorite personality that Dad carried in his tool belt was the sarcastically playful Dad. This personality seemed to erase all the bad he had done and would always get him back in good standings with us, giving him never-ending new beginnings.

He would gleefully pick at and make fun of every movement one us kids made until Mom interjected with, "Marvin, cut it out!"

Mom was terrified of spiders, so he would always buy fake ones and hide them for her to randomly find. This never seemed to get old to me. As Dad was whispering the plan, I couldn't hold back the belly laughs. He would give me the universal sign language of being quiet because we would be in stealth mode, so I would fight back the belly laugh with a quiet snicker.

"Kathy, come here." Mom would hesitantly walk in the room already terrified of someone or something jumping out to scare her.

"Marvin, you had better not have a spider in here."

Our small giggles would have already turned into full blown stomach grabbing laughs and Mom was still in tiptoe mode. We couldn't control the anticipation of her joyful scream. It always sent a wave of enjoyment, creating an avalanche of kids on the floor hee-haw laughing.

"Kathy, hush and grab that pillow. Reluctantly, she would grab the pillow anyway and scream, "Damnit Marvin!"

All of us hee-haw laughing, Dad tickled with mischief, and Mom screaming, "Somebody better get that mess!"

Dad would grab the fake spider and throw it in her direction to incite the riot of laughter.

"MMMMAAAARRRRVVVVIIIINNNNNNN!"

He would look at us and chuckle, sending us into another laughing frenzy, all while quickly removing the evidence right before Mom had enough. He was always such a good gauge of the Mom meter. He knew the precise moment Mom was at her breaking point and would smother the flames of our laughter with his head down and a cocked eyebrow, letting us know we had pushed too far. This was the most exciting part because now we had to fight back the bursts of laughter with muffled snickers between one another. "Ok, Ok boys, calm down. Your Mom has had enough," while he's fighting back laughter with his side smirk inciting our gut wrenching cackles.

We had such a connection with the monster and the man Dad was and wanted to be. All the fear he unleashed on us at Hilltop Drive could all be forgotten as we were lost in his silliness. Dad truly wanted to be the good guy but the Hulk in him had to destroy everything in his path.

Dad was the villain, but was always revered as the good guy, due to his honorable intentions.

"Son, I will never miss any of y'alls events."

Dad was a man of his word when it came to this, and anytime there was a soccer game, karate session, school play, or just us having backyard wars, Dad was there watching and coaching. Even though he was defined by the Hulk rage within him, he was still Dad and I loved Dad so hard.

I loved every side of Dad.

I didn't want to do what Dad did, but I wanted to be Dad.

Dad was my superhero.

It s Our Secret

So many times Dad would encourage me to push just a little harder. To never settle for just the status quo and to never be satisfied with my production, because there is always more.

I am so thankful for this mentality, but as a child, it caused me to face all the difficult complex sides of doubt and self-criticism that led to many dead-end roads.

Dad was a swap meet and flea market type of bargain shopper. He would go through hell and high water to get what he called "the deal." These eventful deals would happen every single weekend, rain, sleet, snow, or sunshine.

Dad would attend multiple flea markets in various cities starting as early as 6am. All these extravaganzas I would partake in firsthand.

"You're my right-hand man, son," Dad would say while grabbing my thigh as we headed to the first of many flea markets to find "the deal."

I'll never understand why Dad chose me, but I knew come 5:30am, I had better be ready to ride.

Scared to ask any questions while we drove, I chose silence until Dad decided to spark conversation. I merely engaged because I was terrified.

I was terrified of Dad because I never knew which version of him I would get.

I didn't know if I would get the immediately angry unknown Dad if I replied with the wrong answer or asked the wrong question.

The other Dad had perfected the cold shoulder, ignoring me if he didn't agree with the current circumstance.

There was also a philosophical Socrates Dad that would expound on a topic he was passionate about with the deepest of insights known to man.

The sarcastically playful Dad would gleefully pick at and make fun of every movement we made until Mom interjected with, "Marvin, cut it out!"

Mom was terrified of spiders, so he would always buy fake ones and hide them for her to randomly find.

"Kathy, come here." Mom would hesitantly walk in the room already terrified of a spider jumping out.

"Marvin, you had better not have a spider in here."

"Kathy, hush and grab that pillow. Reluctantly, she would grab the pillow anyway and scream, "Damnit Marvin!"

Dad laughing and Mom screaming, "Somebody better get that mess!"

Dad would grab the fake spider and throw it in her direction to get the scream he wanted.

"MMMMAAAARRRRVVVVIIIINNNNNNN!"

He would look at us, chuckle, and get us to laugh, but quickly remove the evidence right before Mom turned it from a game to serious.

Because of all the sporadic facets of Dad, the best technique was to not speak until spoken to, which I had perfected.

Much of the first part of the morning ride consisted of my Dad asking random questions as if he were just meeting me for the first time every weekend.

"How have you been?"

"What's been going on?"

"How's school?"

These open-ended questions would have my mind doing a juggling act, so instead of responding, I chose silence.

He would jump back and forth asking me so many questions, but nothing would come out. I would just sit in silence playing the guessing game in my mind of what is the right answer to give. These questions would usually take the first part of highway 11E, an old highway that connected us to the big city, Knoxville.

Seeing the Knox County sign was how I gauged the timing of questioning because once we hit this sign it was like an alert for my Dad to switch to his buying mentality.

Dad would start queuing me on how to approach the owners of the booths if I wanted an item to "Jew down," or get a lower price than what was ticketed.

I loved to see Dad in this element because he was such a chameleon. He could sell salt to a slug or sand to an Egyptian as he would say.

Nothing Concealed: Veiled Secrecy Will Be Brought To Light

Dad was just smooth. There was no way of denying it, and I got to witness it all firsthand.

His technique was flawless. He would laser focus on the item of his desire, knowing the attendant of the booth noticed him. He would play a cat and mouse game of eye glancing and avoiding eye contact to not draw too much attention to the desired item. Then he would let them approach and speak. Saying nothing, he would nod and smile. This was almost a tease to the attendant and, like clockwork, they would give a lower price than what was ticketed. At that point Dad knew he had them, so he would say, "I am just looking," and we would leave.

At this point I felt comfortable enough to talk so I would always ask, "Dad, why wouldn't you just buy it now because it's cheaper?"

He would then go into his hustling philosophies. "Son, you can run down and F one or you can walk down and F them all." I had no idea what he was talking about but went along with it with an over exaggerated head nodding.

"Son, if they offer you a cheaper price right off the bat then be patient, let their anxiousness allow you to take control and you can get whatever you want for the price you call."

He would scroll the flea market spotting the items he wanted like a sniper in the military from a far distance to not tip anyone else off.

As the day was ending, he would make his rounds to the booths where the desired "deals" he sought out the most were. The booth owner would reapproach and before they could even speak, my Dad would give a declaration of how much money he had on him and that he would take the item off their hands now.

The problem was Dad always undervalued the booth owners' ticket price exponentially.

One specific time, my Dad saw a University of Tennessee orange pickup truck that he was eyeing for projects at home. We approached the booth owner and Dad immediately said, "I have $500 cash and will take this off your hands right now."

Well, the ticket price said $1500. I knew Dad had more cash on him but he always acted as if the money he showed them was his last dying dollars and that buying it at his offer was such a great deal for them.

Somehow, more times than not, Dad would walk off with the item he so desired. That day was no different and we left with a UT orange pickup truck.

Looking at me after the booth owner threw him the keys Dad said, "Son, if you tell people confidently what you are going to do, they will let you do it. Stand on what you say."

"Yes sir."

It was endearing to see my Dad meet people where they were mentally no matter their background and hustle.

Because of this, I started to enjoy those flea market weekends, and I think Dad did as well. It gave him an opportunity to teach me while at the same time show off his gift. It was only for me to see and I was thankful for him sharing his special skills with me.

Soon Dad had me doing the hustling. He would give me some cash and send me to the item he desired.

At first, he would be side-by-side with me, almost walking me through his selling 101 foundations class. Eventually, he would sit back and let the magic happen.

I would talk anyone, and I mean anyone out, of what they were selling for cheaper.

"Son, I am so proud of you. I never have to worry about you Jarrod. You're going to be ok."

I had no idea what he was talking about at the time, but he showed a different type of love during these moments and I lived for it. Dad and I became thick as thieves on the weekends with our consistent hustling.

During the week was hell, but I longed for the weekend of affirmation and championing me on for winning his prize possessions. These weekends had been going as planned until one strange weekend.

Dad and I partook in our normal routine of awkward re-getting to know each other as we took the drive down 11E. We passed the Knox County sign allowing us both to lower our guard because we were now in our element of hustling.

Dad would begin the rules of engagement process as a consistent refresher, but at the end of everything, he added a new wrinkle that someone would be meeting us.

Nothing Concealed: Veiled Secrecy Will Be Brought To Light

I thought nothing of it until we arrived. We got out of the car, but Dad became disheveled and was kind of scrambling around for some unknown reason. Then I saw why. I saw her.

She was a middle-aged brunette white woman that was not much taller than me.

I thought of nothing but how this midget lady was taking my time with Dad. This was *our* time to make moves.

The day was so strange because I was an afterthought. Dad wasn't focused at all on any items like usual. When I saw something I thought might interest him, he would kind of shrug it off and go back to conversation with the lady. I never got her name and honestly didn't care because I was focused on the purpose of being there: "the deal" and my time with Dad.

The day was cut short and, on the way home, the cold shoulder technique was in full effect. Usually we would recap the items we got and Dad would go over pointers on how we could've gotten them even cheaper with some minor adjustments. Instead, to my obliviousness, Dad was contemplating what he had done and was preparing an explanation just in case I accidentally mentioned it.

I said nothing because I knew nothing.

The next weekend, our morning routine went normal as usual.

Alarm went off at 5:00am and I knew to be bright eyed and bushy tailed because the train started moving at 5:30am.

Once we got in the car, the atmosphere was different. It was smothering. The hot air was circulating with uncertainty. There was no "You're my right-hand man, son," and the awkward cold shoulder was in full effect again with Dad. Our usual route was changed when Dad decided to head east on highway 11E instead of our normal westwardly bound route.

I was wrestling with confusion, trying to process what was going on but knew this was still the awkward beginning of the trip. I just dropped my head in silence.

Besides the uncertainty engulfing the car, the only other thing prominent was the deafening silence. Dad was obviously contemplating his next moves.

We made another unknown turn. I subtly slid to the edge of my seat to look until my seat belt clicks and locks. I side eyed Dad and we met eyes. He quickly turned his head forward, back to the road.

Even Dad's hand positioning on the steering wheel was abnormal.

He usually drove with his knee, only making sporadic contact with his right hand at 12 o'clock when needing to slightly redirect the wheel.

Today he was focused, with his right hand at 3 o'clock and his left at 9 o'clock. It looked like his hands were jockeying for position on which way to turn but his eyes led the way.

We slowly pull up to an apartment complex. Dad parks. We get out.

He takes immediate lead and I follow.

Head down a few paces behind, we climb some stairs.

We arrive at a door and without hesitation Dad knocks.

The lady from the flea market answers the door.

Then Dad started moving at the speed of light. No words and fast paced walking, they direct me to the couch. With my head still down to not make eye contact with anyone, I see Dad's back moving swiftly down the hall.

"I'll be right back son," and the door shuts very slowly and quietly.

I said and did nothing. All I could do was kick my legs and keep my silence while my brain fought against itself with questions:

Why are we here?

Is he coming back?

Who is the lady?"

Why does she keep stealing my Dad?

What do I do?

While my legs kicked, I started to hear faint noises. My legs stop kicking. I start to lean my body and begin to feel myself falling, so I grab onto the edge of the couch with both hands. I grip tighter, lean more, and can hear the faint sounds start to grow louder.

I straighten up stiff as a board, grip my hands tighter, and squeeze my eyes together as tight as they will go.

At night when I got afraid, I would pull the covers over my head until the fear stopped. I didn't have a blanket, so my eyes became a cover from the darkness surrounding me.

The noises got louder and faster until it abruptly stopped.

I waited a few minutes to open my eyes and when I did, Dad appeared still moving at the speed of light. This time he wasn't accompanied by the lady.

Nothing Concealed: Veiled Secrecy Will Be Brought To Light

He grabs me by the wrist, gripping the life out of it and nudges me quickly to move.

We make our way down the steps to the car and before I realize it, we're back on 11E.

Dad appears to have calmed down but continues the cold shoulder treatment nonetheless.

With his hands back at three and nine o'clock, gripping the steering wheel tighter and clenching his jaw, he sternly says to me "Son, this is our secret."

With my head still down, "Yes sir."

Why was he mad at me?

Did I make too much noise at the apartment?

What did I do?

Fearful I did something wrong, "I'm sorry Dad."

I waited for a response, but the dead silence consumed the car again.

Highway 11E never seemed this long before. Every other Sunday, the time together flew by. But not knowing if Dad was mad at me made this ride home feel never-ending.

We finally got home to our normal full house. Mom, my brothers, and sister knew our ritualistic weekend practices so nothing was different until Mom asked, "How did it go baby? Get anything new?"

Without hesitation, "We went to some ladies house."

Mom turned into a top ranked detective asking me so many questions.

"What was her name?"

"Where does she live?"

"How long did you stay?"

I had no answers.

She became agitated and I spouted out, "Dad left me on the couch."

"DO WHAT JARROD?!"

"Dad left me on the couch and walked down the hall with the lady."

At that moment, I knew I messed up. Mom shrieked, "MARVIN!"

Instant tears erupted from her eyes and she disappeared into the back room.

I was scared because Dad told me not to say anything. He's going to be mad at me now. I won't be able to go to the flea market with him anymore. He's going to whoop me. He's going to take someone else now.

Mom is crying now, so it's my fault. She's not going to want me to go with Dad anymore. She is going to be mad at me.

For what felt like hours, nothing but yells and screams came from that back room.

The yells and screams echoed throughout the house like we were in the deepest darkest cave.

A door swings open and Dad's voice sternly yells,

"JARROD!"

My heart sank.

What did I do?

What is going to happen? Because he told me plainly not to say anything.

He looked at me with eagle piercing eyes, leaned down, jaw clenched, looked me in the eyes and said, "I told you this was our secret, and I can't tell you anything else."

He swiftly walked out of the front door, slamming it behind him.

I was devastated.

I was broken. He hated me now.

What did I do?

Why did I hurt Mom and Dad?

I didn't do anything but answer Mom's question.

I fell to the ground broken. All I could do was cry. Mom came out to console me, "You didn't do anything wrong baby. You did the right thing."

"Dad hates me."

"No, he doesn't, he hates himself."

I wanted to believe her, but she was obviously lying because Dad just walked out mad at me.

Confusion surrounded me on all sides, with no one willing to explain to me what just happened.

My brothers and sister asking me, "What did you do, Jarrod?"

Usually I knew, but this time I had nothing to tell them.

I felt like the game we played as children, monkey in the middle, unknowingly.

Nothing Concealed: Veiled Secrecy Will Be Brought To Light

The mind wrestling starts.

Were all these so-called father son weekends a practice run for this and I failed?

Is Dad coming back?

If he comes back, is he ever going to talk to me again?

Is Mom mad at me?

Why did I say anything? I should've kept my mouth shut and none of this would've happened.

Nighttime caught us and it was time to lay down. There was still no sign of Dad.

Insomnia was my only friend.

I let Mom down.

I let Dad down.

They hate me.

I lay there not knowing what to do.

Lying on my back, looking up towards the popcorn ceiling, I just wanted it all to end.

Bare Knuckle

Skin tattooed in welts pulsating sweat and covered in swollen redness, I clenched down harder on my fist, protruding my bare knuckles even more. Tears sit perched in the corner of my eyes, but I dare not let one drop down my face to avoid the ambush of Dad and Chonci.

Moving my feet in opposite directions to avoid Chonci's closing footwork, my mind starts racing with questions. How did I get here, barefoot on this blistering hot concrete that reflected the blinding sun? Why are we swinging shirtless, barefoot, and bare knuckled at each other's torsos? Why is Dad's face lit up with joy during all of this?

Saturday mornings Cartoon Network came on early and I would be up first to watch tv. But this morning, Chonci decided to use his big brother seniority and take control of the remote.

I was zoned in on Pinky and the Brain until he changed the channel. The first thing I did was slap the remote out of his hand. "You so stupid Chonci. I was already watching this."

"So? I don't care. I want to watch something else," and punched me in the stomach. I did what any other eight-year-old would do and screamed, "MOMMA, CHONCI TOOK THE REMOTE AND I WAS ALREADY WATCHING PINKY AND THE BRAIN!"

Most Saturday mornings, Dad would be outside early fumbling around with stuff until he prepared our daily work plans but today was different. We didn't know Dad was still in the house, hidden in the back room. We heard hard aggressive steps coming down the hall and we both expected it to be Mom. To our surprise it was Dad—and he was angry,

"I'm tired of y'all always fighting and runnin to your Momma to save you," Dad said with his piercing eyes. "Get y'all asses in the basement now!"

The sharp tone of Dad's voice sent chills down my spine because I knew his tone meant somebody was about to get hurt.

Usually, the basement was dark and gloomy but today, it was well lit with the sun penetrating the concrete.

Without making eye contact, "Take your shoes off boys." We reluctantly untied our JC Penny specials looking at one another not knowing what was next. The concrete felt like lava under my feet. When Dad saw I was showing pain from the floor burning my feet he said, "Son suck It up. If you don't mind, then it don't matter."

I bit down on my jaw trying to show Dad how pain didn't affect me.

"Today y'all are going to fight until I get tired."

"Dad, I don't want to fight Chonci."

"Shut up!"

I bit down even harder to avoid any other outburst.

"Boys, y'all are all you have. If you can learn to fight your brother under control then you'll never be afraid to fight anyone else."

Dad started dragging his foot, mapping out a large rectangle that went from the edge of the garage door to the pile of unwashed clothes that lay by the washing machine. Once he marked out the imaginary boundaries, he went into the rules. "You can only hit with the side of your knuckles." He held up his boney black hand demonstrating how to strike our opponent. Dad's pointer and middle knuckles protruded against his skin like they were trying to jump free of his hand. They were huge. I couldn't even focus on what he was saying because I kept examining his knuckles, then mine. He must have realized because with a brisk clap of his hands, I came back to reality.

"Now, take y'all's shirts off and come here." Dad walked us to the middle of the scalding ring like we were preparing for the main ultimate fighting event.

He grabbed both of our wrists and said, "No hitting in the face. Nothing to the head and everything to the body. Make sure you're under control but let your brother know you mean business. Do you understand me.?"

Chonci spoke up first, "Yes sir."

"Jarrod, do you understand?"

Reluctantly, "Yes sir."

Nothing Concealed: Veiled Secrecy Will Be Brought To Light

"Boys, if you lose control, I'll stop it and I'll win the fight. Are you ready?"

"Yes sir."

Facing each other with Dad's hand separating us he yelled, "Hajime!"

Immediately, Chonci moved in for the kill. Splat, my skin screamed as Chonci slammed his side fisted punch into my ribs. It was followed with a burning sensation that felt like when the iron fell on my hand. It was unbearable but I clutched my elbows tighter together to protect my body and locked my tears in the corner of my eyes with a swift head shake.

I retaliated with a splat splat to Chonci's left and right shoulders. Chonci had great blocking technique, so all I could do was try to beat his shoulders up to make him drop his hands. I could tell it hurt when I jammed my knuckles into his right shoulder, so I shuffled my feet like I was going to his left and gave him a devastating slam on his right shoulder again.

Dad yelled, "Great footwork, Jarrod!" Behind Chonci's fists, I could see him grit his teeth in anger as he exhaled like he was preparing to charge like a rabid bull. I knew what was coming so I hunkered down in preparation. Chonci charged, letting his hands fly with all the anger his little body could hold. With each splat of his bare knuckles, what felt like tiny fires followed. One, two, three, four, five, six, seven, and eight shots came, all creating individual pockets of fire all over my body. I was trying to count the punches as they came—eleven, twelve, thirteen—and then I saw stars everywhere. All I could hear was Dad faintly yelling, "Nothing to the head, everything to the body Chonci! Move your feet, Jarrod!"

The stinging sensations went away and I couldn't feel anything but my legs turning to limp spaghetti noodles. It became hard to stand up but I knew if I fell I would have a bigger problem to deal with: Dad. As I fought my legs from wobbling and collapsing, Dad's faint words became smelling salts.

"MOVE YOUR FEET JARROD," pierced my ears, so I began to move my feet as fast as I could.

"KEEP MOVING!"

I kept moving around and the stars began to disappear but the bee stinging punches lit up my body more intensely than ever. I could no longer hold those tears in place and they began to fall.

"JARROD, CONTROL YOUR EMOTIONS!"

I couldn't and didn't care what Dad said anymore. I backed Chonci up against the garage door and started slamming my bare knuckles into his shoulders over and over until he dropped his hands. I stepped back to look Chonci in the eyes and swung with a hard left-right combination, slamming into the left and then right side of his cheeks. He fell to one knee and I stood there over him breathing heavily and crying.

Dad began to laugh and then fought back his laugh with, "I TOLD YOU TO CONTROL YOUR EMOTIONS AND NOTHING TO THE HEAD!"

I stood looking down on Chonci still crying while he just sat there in that kneeling position.

Dad grabbed Chonci by the arm, making him stand. "Look at each other boys."

We both glanced around the room trying not to make eye contact with one another.

"Boys, I told y'all to look at each other, NOW!"

We both stood swollen and sweaty looking at each other, not saying a word.

"Now give each other a hug and say you love one another."

Looking at Dad, "I don't want to."

"I don't care what you want. Do it now or I'm going to whoop both of y'all."

Immediately, we both leaned in and hugged each other tightly. Neither of us wanted to hug it out but made the sacrifice instead of having to wear a swollen butt as well.

"Boys, from now on anytime there is a problem, we are going to get it out like this. If you can learn to fight one another under control then you'll never be afraid to stand up to anyone. It might be hard to hit your brother but learn to love it because you're making each other stronger. Now, get y'alls asses ready to get some yard work done."

I Am Proud of You

Sometimes she would call my name and I would squeeze my eyes tighter hoping it was just a dream and then she would stand in the doorway calling my name in a loud whisper, "Jarrod."

I was using the bathroom, standing there and then I heard the door creak. The Lady was standing there like a dark shadowy cloud. "How's my baby doing?" I say nothing, she turns off the light and slowly shuffles over to me, lowers the toilet seat, sits down, and takes her swollen puffy hand slowly down my pants. "Jarrod." I stay silent and just drop my head. She slowly starts to massage my pee-pee over and over, over and over, over and over.

"Jarrod."

"Do you like this?"

"Yes."

"Good job, baby. Good job. Now, you go back out there, be quiet, don't wake anyone up, and lay back down."

I was a good boy, and she was proud of me. I was a good boy but why did I feel so disgusting? When I see a black woman with those same puffy swollen hands, I still get that feeling. It's like the spider dream that I think every kid has…where you are comatose within that REM sleep and before you know it, one spider scratches the bottom of your foot alerting you to pull up the sheets. Nothing is there. It makes its way up your leg and three more join the party. Mid sleep, thigh smacking, to no avail, the thigh rumble incites the spider community and now thousands are everywhere, consuming your bed and body. You sit up snappily, but nothing is there, so all you can do is curl up in the fetal position and wait it out until the sun's beams shine through the window to kill any remaining shadow spiders. This feeling never goes away and is all consuming when I see those puffy swollen black hands to this day.

It was the never-ending Groundhog Day story with the lady and the old beat-up craftsman style home. It was as if I walked into a black hole daily, packing away anything that happened to me in the deepest darkest places in that cave to never be found again.

One of the last days I can remember in the Lady's house ended in, of course, a spanking for me. It was a Friday and Mom was running late to pick us up. It was payday for Mom and the Lady, so maybe this was planned but I was anxiously awaiting Mom at the busted up front screen door. I think Mom liked to always run late because it gave her an excuse to speed in the "Red Car," and accumulate more speeding tickets. The infamous red car was an old school muscle car. It purred so loud when you revved the engine. I can remember sitting in the passenger backseat getting that inner ear tickle feeling when Mom revved the engine. "Keep an eye out for cops," she would say, "because we're running behind." We always seemed to be running behind but Mom's batman-like driving skills helped us to roll through stop signs, accelerate through red lights, drift semis, and navigate through traffic like a snake through tight fitting rocks. Mom was a dangerous speed demon that gave two demonstrative rules, "SHUT UP AND SIT THE HELL BACK!" I don't ever remember a car seat or hell, even a seatbelt, but do remember feeling like a bunch of gerbils in a cage getting shaken around, but oh how I loved the speed. I would always ask, "Mom can I drive?"

"Jarrod, don't make me pull this car over! Sit your ass back and shut the hell up!"

"Yes ma'am!"

"Watch your attitude. You forget who you talkin to?!"

"Yeeeessssss Maaa'aaM"

After what seemed like hours waiting for her at The Lady's door, Mom finally pulled up. "Mom's here!" I start to run out the door, but I knew that I had better not because that was a whoopin. You had better not run outside without permission and that would've been two double whammies at once, one from the inattentive Lady and one from Momma. So, I anxiously wait for Mom to run up the stairs. No matter what type of day Mom had, she would always change her voice and give you the, "Hey baby, how was your day?" Those words floated out of her mouth and wrapped around you even before her touch would, making any

Nothing Concealed: Veiled Secrecy Will Be Brought To Light

and everything that happened stay buried deeper in that hole. "Good, Momma, it was good."

"It had better be or you know I'll bust that ass." She said it with a smirk that you knew was serious, but she was just as glad to see us as I was to see her. Instead of the normal wadded-up hand-to-hand cash exchange, Mom, with tense body language, told us, "Run to the car kids."

"YES MA'AM!" I was so ready to leave her stankin azz house, so I rushed out hearing Mom in the distance, "Don't touch shit!" As a parent, this is an automatic give away. This means I am about to have some time on my hands. I open the squeaky Red Car door. We all pile in and, within seconds, it's game on. My oldest brother was Honest Abe and made sure to tell me, "Jarrod, you better not mess with nothin because Mom said we better be good."

"Shut up punk." Two jabs to the ribs later, I regrouped and burrowed my way to the front seat. I could see Mom in the raggedy doorway using her Ebonics sign language as usual. When Mom talked with her hands, she was in deep explanation and who knows when the conversation would end. I place myself in the front seat acting as though I am Mom. "Y'all sit down and shut the hell up!"

"Stop that cussing or I am telling."

"I don't give a damn. I'll just drive off."

"Jarrod, I told you to stop messin."

I am adjusting everything from the knobless radio that only had the metal protruding to the purple Indian air freshener that reeked of old lavender hanging on the warped rear view mirror that Mom used to threw blind backhands. I don't know why she never adjusted it but maybe that helped when she was speeding like Night Rider through the city. Nevertheless, I continue to touch wherever my 4'1 reach would reach. Then I saw it, the keys, hanging from the ignition.

"Don't even think about it Jarrod." I pretend to start the car, "vrooooommmmmmmm, vrrooooooommmmmmmm," imagining the tickling sensation I would get in my ears when Mom would press that pedal to the flow. The car was screaming at me, "DRIIIVVVEEEEEEE MMMMEEEEEE, JARRRRROOODDDDDD!" Who was I to deny it, so I started the Red Car. Everyone freezes in fear and the first thing I do is look up at the door. Nothing! Mom is still signing away and lost in her own hand confusion. I shimmy down to the edge of the seat so my feet can touch the pedal. I drive it to the floor. VVVVVVRRRRRRROOOOOOOOOOOMMMMMMM!!!!

"JARROD, STOP, I'M TELLING!" I panic like a bank robber in a heist. I grab the gear shift on the tree and pull it down. We begin to roll backwards. Let me tell you, this was the slowest car theft in the history of car thefts. In that moment, Mom's spidey senses kicked in. I don't know how she knew it was me from the top of my head at the dashboard, but she screamed, "JARROD," kicked that door open and turned into Flo Jo, the most beautiful and fastest Olympian. She got there in what seemed liked two strides and in one fell swoop, she opened the door, put the car in park, and whooped the ever living ish out of me. "DIDN'T. I. TELL. YOUR. DUMB. BLACK. ASS. NOT. TO. TOUCH. ANYTHING!!!!" Tears, yelling, cussing, crying, smacking, yelling, and crying for the longest five minutes of my life. She grabbed me by the arm, slammed me over the seat, looked at The lady and said, "Thank you for everything and these DAMN kids!" I don't know if Mom was more stressed about me almost sending us to a slow rolling t-boning accident or relieved she got out of the nonstop full body explanation to The Lady in the doorway. Nonetheless, with the stern "I want to kill you eyes" look and a single wave out of the car window, we never again stepped foot back into The Lady's house.

Homework

With her jaw clenched and fire boiling in her eyes, Mom quizzed, "If five birds are sitting on a bench, three flies off, and five come back, how many birds are left?"

I could hear the hurt and fear bubbling up in his throat as his voice creaked like the old floorboards in the kitchen as he faintly replied, "Three."

"You damn dummy!" I edged closer on the couch leaning in as Mom's voice started to echo louder with the gurgling of anger rumbling in her chest. "CHONCI, IF FIVE BIRDS ARE SITTING ON A BENCH, THREE FLIES OFF, AND FIVE COME BACK, HOW MANY BIRDS ARE LEFT?" I could hear Chonci's chest pounding and his breaths speeding up. An eruption of tears came out and Chonci yelled, "I DON'T KNOW!"

"You retarded!" I heard the floorboards creak, and I knew I had better play blind, deaf, and dumb, so I slid all the way back on the couch with my legs dangling like nothing was happening. Mom looked at me with snarling disgust, showing her teeth like an angry dog about to attack.

As soon as she disappeared down the hall, I jumped up and ran to Chonci, "It's seven Chonci, the answer is seven." Tears streaming down his face, he looked at me in disgust and said, "Shut up. I hate you."

I heard scuffling in the back room, so I scurried back to my oblivious positioning on the couch, gazing off in the distance as Mom came back equipped.

She had a leather belt in one hand with both ends of the belt in her right hand making a loop, while she was clutching the opposite end of the loop with her left. Looking at me, she put both her hands together and pulled. The belt exploded with a loud pop as the leather ends collided. I jumped and could hear Chonci jump as well because the chair scuffled abruptly across the floor.

I edged closer on my seat leaning in, almost falling off the couch. "I am going to ask you one more time and if you don't get this answer right, I'm going to bust yo ass! Do you understand me?"

With his small voice, "Yes ma'am."

By this time, I am peeping around the corner into the kitchen and see Chunky shiver aggressively like the thermostat suddenly dropped below zero.

"CHONCI, IF FIVE BIRDS ARE SITTING ON A BENCH, THREE FLIES OFF, AND FIVE COME BACK, HOW MANY BIRDS ARE LEFT?"

Chonci sat there in silence. I knew he was contemplating the answer I gave him. I am sitting there mouthing SEVEN to myself. I lean around the corner and Chonci is staring at me. Mom yells, "What the hell is it Chonci?" Without hesitation he says, "Three."

I jumped back throwing myself on the couch confused. Why would he not tell Mom the answer I had just told him? I knew it was right.

"CHONCI GET YOU ASS UP!" Mom striped him with that belt on every word that came out of her mouth. "YOU ARE NOT DUMB CHONCI! STOP BEING STUPID AND APPLY YOURSELF DAMNIT!"

Mom sounded like she was about to cry with each word that came out of her mouth, but it was drowned out with Chonci's yelps of pain.

Yelling at the top of her lungs like I was outside and down the street, like she hadn't just seen me on the couch, "JARROD, GET YOUR ASS IN HERE!" I jumped off that couch with the quickness and in two steps was at the kitchen table.

"Yes Ma'am?"

"Jarrod, you had better tell your brother how many damn birds are left!"

"It's seven, Mom, it's seven."

"Thank you, Jarrod. See Chonci, it's not that damn hard. "Why can't you be like your brother? Jarrod never brings a book home and makes straight A's. What the hell happened with you?"

Chonci is standing, head down, with a panting cry. I lean in to put my hand on his shoulder and he slaps my hand away. "Don't you touch me, Jarrod!" I just wanted to show him I cared and that I was sorry for trying to help. All this did was incite Mom.

"You had better stop that soft ass shit, Chonci! Your brother is only trying to help your stupid ass and you mad at him. Suck those tears up or I'm going to give you something to cry about! You know ain't nothing worse than a soft ass man, so you had better dry it up, RIGHT NOW!"

The thermostat must have dropped again because we both aggressively shivered simultaneously. I began to cry because Chonci was mad at me, "I'm sorry Chonci."

"Don't you start that shit, too! Y'all had better finish this work and clean up before I get back. Do y'all understand me?" In unison, "YES MA'AM."

Mom walked off not making any eye contact with the belt hoisted over her shoulder dangling like Hulk Hogan's WCW championship belt ready to slap anyone with it at any time.

We both waited until the floor creaks were far enough in the distance and Chonci looked at me, "You always kissing ass Jarrod."

"I told you the right answer. Why didn't you tell Mom?"

"Because you are a pussy and I hate you."

"Well, I'm a smart pussy and you retarded."

That's all it took to reignite the fire in Chonci's eyes. He punched me right in the face, connecting with precision his first two knuckles in my eye. He realized it hurt me because no sooner than he punched me, he covered my mouth with his hands. I was sobbing and slobbering in his palms. He clinched his jaw, "You better shut up fag or Momma's coming back in here." Mom must've heard the scuffling around but all she did was yell from her room, "Y'all better be in there working or I'm whooping ass when I get in there!" I didn't need Chonci's hands to muffle my tears anymore because Mom's threat alone dried up my tears.

Eye immediately swollen and snot running, I jumped up on the table to finish Chonci's homework.

"I don't need your help! That's why you're adopted, with your funny ears."

"I might have funny ears, but Mom said you should be like me, smart, you dumbass."

"When we get downstairs, I'm kicking your ass Jarrod."

"Only because you're stupid and I'm smart. I'd rather be beat up and smart than a dummy like you."

Chonci looked around to make sure the coast was clear and gut punched me, reminding me, "You better not cry because Mom will come out here."

All the air deflated out of my body. I couldn't breathe, but he was right, I had to take the pain instead of alarming Mom with my tears and both of us getting whooped until she felt better.

The insults and me getting hit carried on for what felt like an hour and then we heard the floorboards creaking again.

Chonci looked at me and flinched as a warning for me to keep my mouth shut or else. We both stood at attention until the steps on the floor got louder and closer. Heads down as Mom walked in, "Did y'all finish?"

"Yes Ma'am."

"Jarrod, what happened to your eye?"

I slightly looked up and said the obvious, "Nothing, Mom." She accepted that answer and then said what we both hated to hear.

"From now on boys, when you get off that bus, I want y'all two to get your ass to this kitchen table and get your work done together. Jarrod, I want you to help your brother finish his work and then I'll come check it."

That news hurt worse than the sucker gut punch I was still recovering from.

Reluctantly, Chonci and I looked at each other side-eyed, "Yes Ma'am."

"I don't think you understand me boys!"

"Yes Ma'am."

"Now, get y'all's ass in the room!"

Mom didn't care anything about daylight savings time because when the clock struck six it was time for us to start making our way to our rooms and to get the hell out of her face.

"But Mom, it's still light outside."

"But Mom, hell. Don't have me grab that belt and put you to sleep!"

I didn't care about it being light outside, but I knew that since Chonci and I shared a room, there would be hell to pay for the homework debacle.

I had to share a room with Chonci, who was what Dad called anal. I didn't know what that meant but I knew not to touch anything in the room that belonged to him.

We had a wooden bunk bed that sat directly across from the window that got controlled by Chonci. When coming into the room the first thing that would jump out was the light blue dingy carpet that never seemed to get used unless my face was being forced into it by Chonci, due to me allegedly touching something. Perpendicular from the heavy wooden bunk bed was a desk that Chonci monitored hourly. He would have his books and pencils lined up perfectly side-by-side with equal spacing between them. I was an Alcatraz prisoner trapped to the bottom bunk quarters. If I would get up to go pee, Chonci would make noise to alert me he was watching.

With the sun beaming in through the window directly hitting me in the face, there was nowhere to hide. It was too hot to use the fear tactic, where I would pull the covers over my head until the sun decided to go to sleep, and I was hesitant to touch the blinds because of what Chonci would do.

I lay there for what seemed like hours and I just couldn't take it anymore. I jumped up out of bed, rolled the blinds closed, and slapped his pencils out the desk.

Before I could jump back under the covers Chonci met me at the desk.

"Why did you touch my desk?"

"It's not your desk Chonci. Leave me alone and go to bed. You're always trying to run stuff."

I tried to push my way back to my bottom bunk and that's when he saw it. His pencils were on the floor. He grabbed me by my throat and squeezed as hard as he could. I fell on the bed and his grip just got tighter. Usually, with the noise being made Mom would've yelled but there was silence in the house and I couldn't scream. He had a vein that was bursting from his forehead, and he kept saying, "Don't you ever touch my stuff." The more I kicked to get him off me the tighter he squeezed. "Don't you ever touch my stuff again." Fighting for air, I finally got one hand free and struggling to breathe, "Chonci, stop. Please stop." He got both his hands back to my neck and squeezed even harder. I felt the room going dark. "Chonci," is all I could get out and with one last kick, he fell to the floor. Mom heard the thump, "WHAT THE HELL ARE YALL DOING IN THERE? I TOLD YALL TO GO TO SLEEP DAMMIT! IF I COME IN THERE I BUSTIN EVERYBODY ASSES! NOW, GO TO SLEEP!"

Chonci jumped up and looked at me, "Don't you ever touch my stuff again!"

"You are stupid and psycho."

"I'm telling you Jarrod, if you ever touch my stuff again, I'll hurt you!"

"You think you're the boss of me Chonci but you're not."

"Try me Jarrod and see what happens."

"I'm not afraid of you and when we get bigger, I'm going to show you." With that, he jumped back on top of me, punched me at least ten times all over and said, "Well, we not big yet."

I started to cry, and all he said was, "Don't ever touch my stuff again."

"I hate staying in this room, Chonci."

"Well, I hate you and wish you were never born."

"You're just mad because you dumb." He gut punched me one more time to force out the rest of the silent tears, jumped off me, and climbed back to the top bunk. With the sun still beaming in my face, I lay there curled up in a ball, and motionless, watching the sun go to sleep and the darkness wake up.

I lay there, my mind spinning like the clanking washing machine I could hear in the distance. I just wanted to be like my big brother but why did he hate me? What did I do to him? All I could think about was getting off the bus and having to do homework with him. It made me sick to my stomach but the only thing I could do was squeeze my knees tighter to my chest.

I hate living here and I hate my family.

The Jennings Route

Athletics dominated our household.

Football was introduced to me around the age of six but before that we did martial arts every day since I was four years old. Dad was a fifth-degree black belt and had a dojo.

Before each session, we would have to hold an American split, raising our hands out in front forming a triangle, and recite, "See I am an eye, I will not fight unless I have to. Mind first, body second, breathing overall, eternal peace."

This was to instill consistency and discipline or at least this is what Sensei Houston and Sensei Charles Allen would tell us.

Sensei Charles Allen was my Dad's partner who was a black belt as well and had practiced for over twenty years.

I wasn't given an option to participate but knew if I didn't there would be hell to pay. "Discipline and consistency" is what Dad would sporadically yell in the classes to drive his point home.

"Discipline is doing what you don't want to do day in and day out to be great." Great at what, was the problem. Great to Dad was external affirmation from others.

He would tell us congratulations before an event because we had better perform. It was never a good job, but you could do better. Instead of creating discipline at a young age, he created self-critics since it was never good enough for ourselves but great if others outside the home affirmed what we did.

Discipline in the Houston household started with the Jennings route.

The Jennings were a prominent black family that owned a barber shop where all twenty-five-black people in Jefferson City went to get their haircut, men and women alike. They also owned three or four blocks of what we called old downtown Jefferson City.

Old downtown was a collaboration of run-down buildings that were deemed historical, but Lord knows that with one strong gust of wind the four blocks, they would collapse.

We lived on Hilltop Drive that intersected with Rankin street. From there you would make a right on old Chucky Pike heading down a slight hill. At that stop sign, you would cross the street and the Jennings route would begin.

The Jennings route is a designated course created by my Dad. The total route was approximately 2.3 of the longest miles of my life. To this day, if I feel the itch when I am home and start to run it, I can't stop looking at my watch because this road seems to continuously stretch longer and longer.

The first time running this was, let's just say, an experience.

I have only seen my Dad wear shorts a few times in my life and one of those was during this experience. Dad was short and lean but obviously had body image issues when it came to his legs. I say this because when he wore those little Riddell shorts a few times and I remember he would wear white tube socks that seemed to reach so high they turned into a turtleneck. Once those tube socks touched his neck, he would slightly push the bottom down to create a stylish sock crunching fashion statement of sorts.

I was so enthralled in his fashion statement, I got yelled at because I wasn't stretching.

"Jarrod, what the hell are you doing?

Get to stretching!"

How could I stretch? I was amazed that he would create this fashion statement just to run a loop.

We walk to the starting line, the mailbox.

"Jarrod, reach down and touch your toes a few times."

"Yes sir."

He gives me a head nob, looks at his watch, and screams, "GO!"

He takes off like a lightning bolt. At the very beginning, I am giving it my all but in only what feels like twenty-five paces, my legs feel like a baby giraffe. Dad is nothing but high knees and high fashionable tube socks. I am in his distant rear-view mirror now and I am starting to panic. Not one time did he look back, only screamed,

"PUSH, IF YOU DON'T MIND THEN IT DON'T MATTER!"

He finally turns down the hill, never looking back, yelling, "STAY ON THE SIDE OF THE ROAD!"

I've never run any long distance let alone with the traffic.

What do I do?

Do I stop or keep going?

I had to keep going because I didn't want to disappoint him or get in trouble. So, I kept running until I got to the stop sign. Thank God for that stop sign because it gave me time to jog in place and breathe. Waiting for me, he takes a couple of jogs in places and says without looking down, "You better sprint across this street because traffic is coming."

He shoots out like a cannon. I quickly look both ways and give it all I have to cross those two lanes of traffic. I made it but now the run is just now beginning. There is a slight incline of a hill that we start to ascend. This isn't bad in my head and then before you know it Dad yells, "PUSH!" I take off trying to mimic his high knee technique but all I can do is grimace my face and fight the air with my arms going back and forth across my body.

I can't catch him and start to hyperventilate. Never looking back, "Control your breathing!"

Now I am fighting everything, my breathing, arms, this concrete beneath my feet, and Dad's voice.

At that moment, I started to quietly cry because I didn't want him to hear me from two hundred plus yards ahead. I took a deep breath, looked to my right and saw the one place that would have an effect on me at some point in a future Jennings route. I saw a small bridge that had been painted blue only on the top of it and I could hear the creek, Mossy Creek, running below. I continued to quietly cry with the tears flowing but I never stopped moving my feet. We finally made it to downtown and I learned the halfway point was a left at the railroad tracks that went straight uphill. Once you made this left uphill, you would run by a noncompeting white barbershop that had slow moving staple candy cane in front.

There always seemed to be a guy sitting in the chair talking. I can say, I never saw any hair being cut on my many runs, but I always wondered what was so engaging that the person in the seat would be twisted around like an owl talking to the barber, while he was just holding shears. Nonetheless, they would acknowledge us with a head nod and the run continued. At the top of that mountain, there was a stop light. We would make another left, passing the post office on our right, an old bookstore on our left, and a few other buildings that were a never-ending carousel of businesses that couldn't seem to sustain themselves long enough in the old city to prosper.

By this part of the run, I was coasting, had regrouped and was looking and waving at the passerbyers until I heard the sharp pitched whistle my Dad made that could be identified and heard miles away. "LET'S GOOOOOO!"

There was hope now because it's all downhill. I'm feeling the breeze while leaning back fighting the pavement to slow myself down to not fall. Dad's knees aren't that high now either so he could keep himself from falling down this steep hill as well.

We are now at the last two turns and Dad is jogging in place waiting for me to approach. But when I finally get there, he nods without looking at me and shoots out. He's running as hard as he can, so I chase him. As soon as I feel the cramp wiggling up my side, Dad starts yelling, "PUSH, ALL THE WAY TO THE HOUSE!" I'm overwhelmed now, the house is so far away, I am cramping. I can't hold back the tears. I start crying out loud. I know he can hear me because he speeds up.

Why would he leave me now?

He speeds up even more and yells, "YOU HAD BETTER COME ON!" That was the voice I was terrified of, so I ran as hard as I could crying out loud until I reached the finish line at the mailbox.

Once we finished, he didn't say good job or anything, he just put his hand on my shoulder slightly and said, "Be ready because we will run this a lot more."

Still slightly panting and crying, I looked up at him expecting something but what came out next was what defined my Dad. "Suck up those tears and get it together before you come in this house."

It took me a while to come into the house because all I needed was a good job or I'm proud of you, but nothing. When I finally entered the basement door, he was stretching. He slightly lifted his head, looked out the top of his eyes and gave me a slight head nod.

This was my rite of passage, I guess you could say, for what stands to this day in the Houston household as the Jennings route.

Now at Home

"Son, what is your problem?" I wanted to look Dad in the eyes and tell him, "You! You the damn problem, I hate you, and wish you would leave," but it would've probably been ignored as if I said nothing and led to some of his normal catch phrases: "Son, you move slower than two old people copulating" or "You had better get some pep in yo step or ima tighten you up."

Dad was like a broken thermostat when it came to his emotions. You could never tell where he was set but definitely knew when he was too cold or hot. Dad was a type-A person that if you didn't do it like he wanted but still completed the job, it infuriated him. From the way I started my day, cleaning my bed was a potential for his fury to erupt.

"Son, you snap the sheets first, run your hand over to remove all the wrinkles, fold the corner under like a present and tuck it to the middle of the bed. Make sure you start your day off by accomplishing something."

In my head, "Start my day off by spending this much time on making my bed, to mess it back up tonight?" Stupid is what I thought but, "Yes sir," rolled off my tongue because I knew any lip back could create a natural disaster that would affect us all.

Dad was always home but never present. He was always preoccupied with staying busy. Maybe to control his uncontrollable anger or to keep us on task. Dad always said, "If you stay busy, then you won't have time to get in trouble." I didn't need to be busy to keep me out of trouble, I only needed the thought of him talking then whooping me to shiver in fear.

Dad was a no-nonsense type of man that had to be, he said, because his Dad wasn't around. He was second to youngest of six children and was taught to be regimented to avoid trouble. His mother, my grandmother, who I never met, was a strong black woman that didn't take crap from anyone. She had to be strong to raise three boys in the 1950s. Dad always seemed to be reaching for perfection in everything he did, but when he came up short would explode like a volcano and his rage, the lava, destroying everything in his path.

I would soon start to feel the same at home with a different struggle. Now at home, the abuse was not sexual, but mental and physical.

We, my brothers, sister, and I, huddled close in the corner of my sister's daybed hearing screams of terror from the next room over. It was normal to hear arguing every day in the house but today was worse. Bodies hitting the wall, hands smacking flesh, pleas of "Stop Marvin, Please," deep inhales, and thuds with excruciating exhales echoed through the house. We drew closer together, all of us wanting to move but frozen. We all cried softly because we didn't want to alert anyone that we heard, but how could you not? Thirty minutes pass, an hour passes, and nothing, no one has come out of the room. We stare at each other, but no one breaks silence. Then an explosion on my sister's door—BANG— and Dad enters furious. We grip each other tighter but he says, "Shay, get in this room with you mother." All huddled together holding her hand, we had to let go. All crying but nothing we could do except pull closer and cry harder. She dropped her head, let go of our hands, and did as she was told. Yelling erupts again and now we can hear the blows to my Mom repeatedly. "Marvin, please let Shay leave. This is my fault not hers."

"Shut up, Kathy!"

"Don't end up like your mother, Shay! Do as you're told! Do you understand me?"

"Please, Marvin, Please!" Dad becomes even more irate because Mom is pleading to let Shay out of the room.

"Do you want her to be like you?!"

"No, Marvin, No! I'm sorry!"

Sitting there paralyzed by every blow we heard and every echoing scream, we could do nothing. Not knowing what to do, we are petrified and helpless. We contemplate going into the room, but we can't hold him back. Another thirty minutes goes by and my sister comes catapulting out of the room. No words, just head down, tears in her eyes, as she just stands there. At that moment, I felt the same gut wrenching feeling that I had always felt at the babysitter's.

Nothing Concealed: Veiled Secrecy Will Be Brought To Light

There were many more days, weeks, and even years of this repeated yelling, hitting, screaming, and crying, but none stuck out as much as this time. Maybe I realized the word abuse without even knowing the true definition but like the day in the babysitter's house, I too knew this was wrong. Many days, Mom would wear sunglasses to hide the bruises, swollen eyes, and busted eyebrows with the makeup touch-ups around her cheek bones and neck. It was becoming all too familiar. As the opportunities grew for our babysitter and their companions to exploit us, it seemed as though the same was happening at home. I began to fight with every ounce of my being. The most kid friendly agreements turned into all-out war.

"Jarrod, I was watching Gargoyles."

"It's almost over and you've seen this episode a million times. The gargoyle swoops down to stop the bad guy and Tale Spin is on."

"Don't touch the remote."

"You don't own it Chonci!"

"Touch it and see what happens."

There was an unwritten rule in our house amongst the kids, "Nothing to the head, all to the body." You never punched each other in the face because that just meant you wanted to hurt them.

"It's not yours and you ain't gna do nothin."

No sooner than I reached for the remote, I was on my back with an excruciating pain from the side of my eye. I reach up and touch it, "Chonci, I am bleeding!"

"I told you not to touch it." Tears never thought to come to my eyes. I absolutely lost it. Rolling around the downstairs concrete floor, kicking and punching each other as if we were two passing strangers in the street that had an altercation. The fight lasted for what seemed like 30 minutes. We ended up by the garage door, sitting and looking at each other in utter confusion.

"You missed Tale Spin."

"I know."

"Let's hurry up and clean up this blood before Mom and Dad get home." In scrambling to clean up, we kind of side eyed each other and mumbled, "Sorry."

Everywhere I turned, there was something that caused me to hit first and ask questions later.

Sam, our bus driver, must have had these similar problems at his house because I should have been "town student", instead of the permanently nominated front seat passenger. Town students were what most of the "rich" kids were: get dropped off by their Moms and not have to ride the bus. They had to be rich because they would get dropped off right before the bell to homeroom and picked up right at 2:30pm. Who doesn't have to be at work before eight? And they never seemed to be in a rush to go anywhere without having a mask on. I called women that wore a lot of make-up a mask because they never looked the same when they came back to pick them up at 2:30pm. They all looked like they shopped at West Towne Mall's Dillards Mac counter before returning.

Just in the one-hour trip to school, it was common that I had uppercut or kneed a kid for making fun of our house smell or the obviously rotated clothes that my oldest brother had worn a day or so before. Sam would always have a dip of Copenhagen in, knowingly breaking the rules of the no tobacco policy sign that looked you in the face upon entering the bus. He would hide his spit cup by his left leg. I had a great front seat view from the inside crack of the seat.

"Ja-rod, how you this mo-nin?"

"Whatever Sam."

"Heee-Heee, somebody got up on the wrong side of the bed."

"I am fine."

The long ride started off normal with Sam leaning over at each stop sign or railroad crossing to secretly spit in his bottle and then all hell broke loose. I could overhear someone saying, "You stink Chonci." Without hesitation, I got up, ignoring Sam's warnings, "Sit down while the bus is moving," walked up to Spencer, an older punk kid that always tried to be cool, and gave him a three piece, hot and crispy. A hot and crispy three piece meant I threw three fast and hard punches, that connected popping with every blow. Spencer balled up in a fetal position immediately and went crying. Sam stopped the bus abruptly, jolting all the kids around, quickly unfastened his seat belt, and moved his 6'6 skinny frame down the bus. He got to me and assessed the damage.

"Hell, Ja-rod, I told ye to sit down."

When violence happens on the bus, after the ride is over, you go straight to the principal's office and await the dreadful call home. I knew I had screwed up because Mom was going to have to leave work to take me back home. That's a triple ass whoopin. Mom's going to whoop me when she gets there, then again when we get home because she's going to get the dreaded pink slip from work that she always threatened us better not happen, and the worst was Dad would find out and bust me up. Sam obviously saw the fear of God in eyes, so he looked at Spencer and said, "You bet leave these Houston's alone," grabbed me by my arm and gave my personal escort back to my earned front seat. He gently pushed me to the inside of the seat, buckled back up, connected eyes with me in the rearview mirror, got on the intercom and said, "calm down" and took off like a flash to make up time in his route. We got to the school and I knew the inevitable was soon to happen. I sat there with my head down letting everybody get off the bus first. The last kid gets off the bus, I wait a minute to hear the words, "Come on and let's go see Mr. Nolen," but it was different. Without a word, I stand up, raise my head, make eye contact with Sam in the mirror. He gives me the downward head nod. The downward head nod means so many things in a country white town: howdy, nice to meet you, thank you, and you better get on. I knew that head nod meant, "You better get on," so did exactly just that. I entered Jefferson Elementary as one of the Untouchables with the kids asking me what happened. I knew for the safety of myself and Sam, I had better lie and make up the worst possible scenario: paddling—I got 10 licks from Mr. Nolen. From that day forward, Sam and I had an unspoken understanding that what happened on the bus stayed on the bus.

Things got to the point where I only talked with my fist and feet. I didn't care what the kids said, "Jarrod is mean, he likes to hit," or what the teachers said, "Jarrod is great at schoolwork but he's a troublemaker." Because I was the one out of all the siblings to lash out at school, the whoopings at home started to pile on daily and I didn't care.

"Jarrod, do you want to stay in trouble every day?" Mom would ask, walking out of our shared room at night. Chonci would always have something to add, "You need to start listening, Jarrod." This would usually lead to a nighttime quiet ass whoopin with Mom gritting her jaw and talking through her teeth as she's smacking me, "Don't have me get you Daddy up." That's all it took to hit the snooze button on our last argument of the day. The more I got whipped at home, the more attention I got, but the more I wanted to fight at school and the more I wanted to hurt people. There was nothing wrong with that because it happened at the babysitter's and home now, right, but I could never say anything to anyone. Not one time did a teacher, principal, or adult ever ask, "Is everything ok at home Jarrod?" They just assumed I was a bad kid from a "good" family because we were coached up damn good at keeping it between our four walls.

The "pep talks" happened only so often but I knew why they would happen. Dad would have taken his hitting and yelling too far the previous day. I would know sit down pep talk was coming because Mom would get some type of gift that was obvious she didn't want, like flowers or perfume. If it was really bad, Dad would pull out the waterworks, "Kathy, I do this because I love you and I want the best for us. I can't live without you or the kids." This would lead to us being sat down by Dad on the blue oversized sectional in the living room. Dad was like the Boogeyman. He lived on fear and fear alone. He would start out by sitting us really close on that oversized sectional, making us uncomfortable. He would do this stare where he would open his eyes as wide as he could, to where you saw all the whites of his eyes, look down at you, and not blink. It was horrifying and would freeze and melt you in your tracks no matter where you were at. Time was frozen like his glazed over stare and right when you thought he would blink he would start, "Kids, I love you and you Momma, and I want you to know I would do anything for you. I try so hard to show you how much I love you and nobody seems to acknowledge it. I love you more than anything in this world and would do anything to keep us together." Opening his piercing eyes even more, slowly moving his head back and forth like a small oscillating fan, "This is why, WHATEVER. I. MEAN. WHATEVER. HAPPENS. IN. THIS. HOUSE. STAYS. IN. THIS. HOUSE. DO. YOU. UNDERSTAND. ME?" Paralyzed by fear, no one responds, "DO. YOU. UNDERSTAND. ME?"

In unison, "Yes sir!"

I knew the abuse that we were enduring was wrong, but you did as you were told, "Shut the hell up and say nothing!" If there were ever a time I could divulge evidence to a friend, teacher, or just anyone that would listen, all I could see was Dad's glazed over piercing eyes in my mind.

I was a prisoner in my own home and Dad was the evil warden. At any moment, the wrong look or word could erupt into a full-blown fight and have us

Nothing Concealed: Veiled Secrecy Will Be Brought To Light

on lockdown for days. At least the feelings I had at the babysitter's would go away and be forgotten when Mom swooped in to rescue us after work. But the Houston Insane Asylum started to consume all my thoughts with hurt and anger. Every padded wall was a memory of Mom getting slapped, punched, and kicked. The floor was a reminder of my helplessness, being curled up in a fetal position, the ceiling a representation of being closed in from the outside world, and the straitjacket trapping all my emotions inside. "I can't breathe or move! Somebody HEEELLLPPPP MEEEE!"

Coach Scott

Where do I go? What do I do? I was at my wits end. Emotionally, I felt like an egg that had been dropped on the floor: busted with yolk and egg white splattered all over the ground.

With no hope in sight, Dad randomly had my brothers and me load up in the van. We were terrified — well, at least I was. We drove about ten minutes and ended up near our local middle school. He opened the Ford two-tone brown Aerostar door and said, "Get out!"

At first, I thought he was done with us and was just ready to do the dump and abandon move we had seen on many Unsolved Mysteries shows.

I hesitantly stepped out of the van first. I began to look around. In awe, I saw kids everywhere…and they all had on football gear. My Dad was a martial artist and a boxer, so football wasn't a sport we were used to.

I walked down what seemed like a mountain of a hill to get to the field.

"What are y'all waiting for?"

Confused and scared, we stood there not knowing what to do.

He asks again, "What are y'all waiting for?"

We knew that meant MOVE! We took off running, not having a clue where to go but we just ran.

I had the largest butterflies in my stomach, being pushed into an unknown world. There were kids my age to play with, but they were all wearing equipment that was half hanging off them with adults standing around yelling at them.

While we were running a coach yelled, "Boys, get y'all's asses over here!" He looked so disheveled, hat cocked sitting sideways on his head, high tube socks that were stained to high heavens, Riddell single button shorts that were pulled to his belly button, scruffy beard, yellowish brown teeth, a huge—and I mean huge—dip in his bottom lip, and a whistle that stayed spinning around his pointer and middle finger.

I didn't know what to expect because he cussed like a sailor and I didn't even know his name. "What in the hell are you doing?" I turned my head quickly around, looked him eye to eye and dropped my head. "Come here son."

I walked up to him terrified because this was dejavu. Nothing has changed. An adult that screams and yells at me. He just wants to punish me.

Something different happened. He took a knee and looked me in the eye. I can smell the minty (what I learned later was Copenhagen tobacco) all over his breath. He put his hand on my shoulder and side smiled. At that moment, I was safe, at home. I still didn't know this stinky white guy's name, but I wasn't scared.

He lifted my chin with his two whistle fingers and with that side smile and said, "I'm Coach Scott." He pointed with his crooked finger and said, "That's Bean."

I still didn't know what was going on, but he asked me a question that changed my life, "Do you want to play for the Jefferson City Bulldogs, and do you want to hit people?" My eyes lit up and I emphatically said, "YES!"

Of course, Coach Scott thought I was talking about playing for the Bulldogs but all I really wanted to do was hit people. No pads, no cleats, and zero idea what the game of football was, I gave my word to a half scary unknown white man that I would be back the next day to hit people.

Nothing at home mattered anymore: the screaming, yelling, fights, or the fear. Nothing.

My mind was set on tomorrow.

I tossed and turned all night long thinking about what football could be.

Would I be in a gauntlet of non stop hitting, where everyone gets a chance to run me over?

Would I get punished for not wanting to hit people bigger than me?

Are there rules?

How many rules do I have to learn?

What if I can't learn the rules?

What if I get picked last?

Will people laugh at me if I mess up?

I tossed and turned fearful that I would let Scott down. I didn't want to go anymore, so I sat up scared of all the possibilities.

I tried to wait the next day out by staying up, hoping that it wouldn't come.

It didn't work and the light was upon me through the uncovered basement windows.

I had gotten myself so worked throughout the night that I had diarrhea.

Sitting on the toilet, I could hear Dad laughing from his room.

"Jarrod, you, ok?"

"Yes sir, but my stomach hurts."

"You just nervous.

Don't be.

Just listen to the coach and have some pep in yo step."

"Yes sir."

After I got off the toilet, the day moved at light speed. Before I knew it, Dad was yelling, "Let's go boys!"

We loaded up in the van and were off.

Between the late night what ifs and the diarrhea, my stomach was keeping up with the BG's: bubble guts. I was nauseous and filled with excitement all at the same time.

Dad was talking the entire ride but all I heard was "Blah blah blah blah," because I was stuck on the word I gave to Coach.

Practice was late and the dark usually caught us on the field, but Dad opened that two-toned Aerostar van door and said, "If you're on time you're late, so hit the ground running boys."

Timidly tiptoeing through the van Dad yelled again, "Boys!"

I knew that no matter how terrified I was, when my feet hit the ground, I had better be full speed running to coach with a "yes sir" attitude.

Obviously, the day before my nerves had deserted me because that grassy mountain was only a small hill. I did a double take while I was running to make sure my eyes hadn't deceived me. They had — it was only a small hill with high itchy grass.

Coach seemed to be what felt like five miles away, but with our tiny strides we finally reached him.

As soon as we approached him, he said, "Damn, y'all fast." He looked at Bean and slightly gave him a head nod as he was spitting brown minty stuff out of his mouth.

"Y'all early, hell let's get to work."

He had us follow him on another tour to an old white building.

There was an old random toilet, stained brown and black, being used as the door stomp. "Come on boys."

Without hesitation, I walked inside the gloomy half-lit bathroom that had been transformed into an equipment room.

It reeked of mildew and old cut grass. The smell was like a lawnmower that had mowed wet grass multiple days and not been cleaned from underneath. The mildew had a tangy earthy damp dirty sock smell that was pungent to the noise.

It didn't matter to me because Coach was grabbing helmets and jamming them on my head until he found a fit. The only way I knew it was a fit because he did that side glance, spit on the floor, and smacked me upside the head.

"Hell, thisa one isa fit."

Dang that hurt but it seemed right.

I'm walking around the dingy converted bathroom with a helmet on my head. The smell is now more aggressive because it's all concentrated under my helmet.

Next comes the thingy that clips onto my helmet, which I later found out to be the chinstrap. Then Scott grabs some shoulder pads and brings them around my neck. He looks around quickly, grabs a football cleat, and takes a shoelace out of it. He weaves the laces through the shoulder pad holes, attaching both sides of the pads together. Giving an extra tug at the used laces he says, "We gota 'nother fit boy."

I'm standing there with a stinky helmet, shoulder pads, and a willing attitude for whatever is next as Coach begins looking around for something else.

Not knowing what he's looking for, I start following his eyes to see what he might be examining. His eyes perk up and we both see what it is. A dingy pair of used-to-be-white pants with pads in them. They looked as though someone had just used them and put them back, but I didn't care.

"Here, put em on top of your shorts."

"Yes sir."

I begin to scramble with all the other equipment flopping around trying to put the pants on. I got one leg in before he held me from the back of my pants to help me get the other leg in. Once both legs were in, he pulled hard like he was starting a lawnmower. My feet came off the ground, but it situated me into those pants fitting me better. My shorts bunched up uncomfortably but it didn't bother me because I had a full football costume on.

"Am I ready?" He looks me up and down and without a word, shakes his head, bends down, knocking stuff out of the way, and grabs a pair of cleats. He had to secretly be a seamstress because with one glance up and down, he grabbed a pair of cleats that fit like a charm.

With his crooked Copenhagen-stained finger, he pointed in the direction of the field.

No words, I took off as fast as I could.

Leaving that locker room smelling like a dead animal was one of the proudest moments of my life. The smell blanketed and consumed me from head to toe, but I reeked of love.

I was football ready!

I turned the corner running with pads flopping and reeking of musky old equipment.

The grassy hill became a mountain again.

I stumbled over the old but new-to-me cleats and fell from the top, bouncing all the way to the bottom. My little body tumbled until it came to an abrupt halt.

I jumped up holding my pants in one hand and never missed stride until I reached the fifty-yard line.

Curiosity, exhilaration, and anticipation were all over my body the first day of practice. Oh, how I loved the feeling and never wanted it to go away.

The next three days didn't go so well.

Coach Scott had us hit nonstop the first three practices.

"Boys, you gta get o'er the fear first, and then we can play ball."

I felt like an over tenderized T-bone steak. My whole body was sore from the top of my head to the soles of my feet.

One thing was for sure though, I wanted to go back, I wanted to do it again and again.

Because of my love for hitting, Coach Scott Hill, who later became Scott, took a liking to me.

One day he pulled me to the side and said, "Jarrod, call me Scott."

I had never called an adult by anything other than Sir, Ma'am, Mr., or Mrs., so I was terrified, but I respected his wishes. But when my parents were around, I would call him Coach Scott and he would give me that side grin and spit that brown minty juice as to acknowledge he understood.

This so-called game of football came quickly to me. Lord knows it wasn't due to my size because, second to Chonci, I was the smallest on the field. But I had a trait that the majority of other kids didn't have: fearlessness.

I would hit anyone at any time. The harder I hit, the more the coaches and crowd screamed. I loved to hurt people by what Scott and my Dad would call "legally hurtin people."

I would lower my head, close my eyes, and hit with reckless abandonment. The pain was instant but fleeting. The power I felt from hearing a kid scream, to run over a bigger kid, or just flat out hurt someone seemed to last a lifetime.

"Jarrod, you a damn headhunter."

"Keep finding the ball and hitting it son!"

"Yes sir."

I wanted nothing more than to impress Scott. I loved how he would scream at the top of his lungs when I hit someone. Scott was my human thermostat. I could glance over any time during practice and could tell how I was doing by the redness in his face. He would build up like the mercury in the thermostat until he saw an exciting or bad play and would explode letting us all know his immediate temperature. I loved Scott for that. I loved his passion for us and the game of football.

Glimmer of Hope

Every Saturday football game, we would run out to "Bad to the Bone" by George Thorogood and the Destroyers.

The theme of "Bad to the Bone" echoed daily in the background of our practices and we owned it as a team. Teams all around feared the hard-hitting Bulldogs with the fast Houston brothers. We ended our first season undefeated and in the Superbowl with the Pigeon Forge Tigers.

It was a cold Saturday with people littering the stands covered in blankets and shaking their cow bells.

Dad always stayed planted on the track prepared to run the field with any kid that made a long dash for the end zone.

Fans screaming, cow bells ringing, and "BBBBBB Bad to the Bone" playing—on multiple bumpboxxes strategically placed throughout the stadium to remind us we were the Bulldogs—was the setup of my first Super Bowl.

Cold chills consumed me, not because of the below freezing weather but being present enough to feel the love of the fans helmet slaps and pregame congratulations.

Mom had me stuffed in my pads like a pig in a blanket. I had sweatpants under my pads and a sweatshirt that was tucked under my helmet. Warmth wasn't the problem—it was being able to move. Dad had me demonstrate to him that I could move by giving me a few warmups.

"High knees Jarrod."

"Yes sir"

"Tapioca,

Now sprint down to that tree and back."

After I was able to show I could move in my full body sleeping bag, it was time to go.

Scott and Bean called everyone up in the end zone.

"Boys, y'all came a long way in a short time.

Let's kick their asses today and show them we Da Bulldogs!"

Fans, players, and coaches erupted with excitement. We were jumping, yelling, and pushing each other as though we had already won.

Bean raised his hands to hush the crowd.

"Boys, if y'all win, I'll cut my rattail."

Everyone erupted with excitement again.

Bean had a rattail he was proud of. It reached down the middle of his back and was perfectly braided. He would whip it back and forth like a horse would its mane. We knew for Bean to put his infamous rattail on the line, he wanted us to sell out and give our all.

After Bean's speech, he turned the floor over to Scott.

Scott wasn't a big speech type of coach, but this night was special. He pulled us in and once we got close, he said, "Closer boys!"

He hunkered over, cocked his mouth, inhaled deep, and spit a large brown glob of Copenhagen out of his mouth.

He started off in almost a whisper that made everyone lean in even more to listen.

"Boys, it's time to play some damn football."

"Fly around and hit somebody's asses!"

He started getting louder and louder. The anticipation gripped everyone. He started yelling and spit caked up in the corner of his mouth.

"This is our field, so let's send these boys home a cryin!"

"WOOOOOOOO!"

We erupted again. Fans, coaches, and players having a pow wow in the visitors end zone.

Scott came over to me in all the chaos, pat me on the helmet, looked me in the eyes, and in the calmest voice said, "It's time."

Scott was my savior. Savior from home. Savior from trouble and myself. Scott wasn't just my coach—he was my football Dad. Anytime I needed encouragement, all I had to do was look over to the sideline. He was there ready to meet me eye-to-eye and give me the side smirk and head nod needed for encouragement to go just a little bit harder.

Nothing Concealed: Veiled Secrecy Will Be Brought To Light

The other team was bigger, older, and faster than us, but we were "Bad to the Bone."

"Everybody up on me!"

"Who are we?"

... "Bulldogs!"

"Who?!"

... "Bulldogs!"

"Leave it all on the field boys!"

"1, 2, 3"

... "Bulldogs!"

We broke that huddle and headed to the sideline for the game to start.

Every coach made it a point to slap every kid in the helmet and whisper something to them.

It was time to give it all I had. I practiced every day anticipating game days on Saturdays to avoid the life that awaited me outside this rectangle field, and it was time for me to leave it all on the field.

The first quarter was a dog fight. It was 7-7 and kids were getting hurt left and right.

Kids lay on the ground by the bench and crying, scared because Pigeon Forge is too big. Dad sat behind our bench on the sideline and every time I glanced over at him, he was pointing to his head and heart.

Dad would do this to remind me to keep my heart and mind in everything I do.

At the end of the first quarter, I got a 48-quick pitch, broke a tackle in the backfield and ran thirty yards for the touchdown. Immediately, I turn and look for Scott where I found him waving his hat in the air screaming, "YYYEEEEEEEEEEEEE!"

"BBBBBBB Bad, Bad to the bone," blared on the bumpboxxes louder than ever. To overpower our song, cow bells shake the stadium and drown out our fans.

We were up 14-7. After the kickoff, they marched down the field to tie it up: 14-14.

We got the ball back and fumbled.

They went right back down the field and score, 21-14.

I ran to the sideline crying. It's over.

Scott grabbed me by my face mask, "Get your ass in the game. Go get the ball!"

They kick off but we run out of time and at half, it's 21-14 them.

At halftime Bean and Scott are pacing. I couldn't take my eyes off him because I didn't want to let him down.

"Boys, y'all gta leave it on the field.

Y'all gta ATTACK!"

During this time, Dad brought me and Chonci up together and said, "It's time, now get your head in the game!" He pointed to his head and slapped his chest hard.

"Pigeon Forge gets the ball this half, so let's show em who we are.

Who are we?"

… "Bulldogs!"

"Who?"

… "Bulldogs!"

"1, 2, 3"

… "Bulldogs!"

We broke the huddle and headed to the sideline. We kickoff. From the beginning of the half, we dominated on defense. We stopped them every time they got the ball. On offense though, we had no answer. We went three and out every possession.

It is 21-14 them and no one can find any offense.

I heard my name over the loudspeaker almost every play. I am hitting kids in the backfield, on the sideline, and breaking up passes. On offense, they are shutting us down. Nothing will work.

"Timeout!"

It's the fourth quarter and we are losing by 7 and coach brings us in close.

"This is it boys!"

He calls the play. "Jarrod, 48 slot reverse. Go score son!"

I look at Scott and he reassures me with his half smirk and the extra-large discharge of Copenhagen.

He slaps everyone in the helmet and screams, "BLOCK!"

We head out to the field and I get set up in my position.

Nothing Concealed: Veiled Secrecy Will Be Brought To Light

The ball is snapped, and I take off. The quarterback hands me the ball. I look up and Chonci is in front of me leading the way. I see Dad jumping and screaming, pointing to the end zone. I turn the corner, and no one is there. Chonci still leading the way, I gallop into the end zone. The stadium becomes consumed with bull horns from nowhere and "Bad to the bone" blaring. It's deafening.

Dad is pointing and screaming. My team surrounds me in the end zone, and everyone is euphoric with excitement. Slapping helmets and hugging, the referees break it up for the extra point.

In the huddle, coach calls my number again. The play was 12 and I ran straight up the middle.

Dad pointing to his head and heart, the fans screaming, the ball is snapped. I go straight up the middle and jump forward. The refs blow the whistle and throw their hands up in the field goal position, signaling that I scored.

The stadium erupted with emotion again expressed through bull horns and bumpboxxes blaring "BBBBBBBB Bad to the bone."

The whistle blew for the end of intermission.

The game was over 21-21.

I run to the sideline and Scott picks me up and squeezes the life out of me with excitement. I didn't want that hug to end.

What happens next?

The referees call everyone to the middle of the field and explain that there will be overtime until someone is declared the winner.

We win the coin toss and choose our end zone where all our fans are to start overtime.

Coach brings us up with spit fire in his eyes, "Hell, it's time to show them we the damn bulldogs!"

He takes a long inhale and spits out the largest brown spit I've ever seen.

"1, 2, 3"

… "Bulldogs!"

We head to the field and the ref lines the ball down at the ten-yard line.

We have four tries to score, whether it be a touchdown or field goal and then the other teams have the same opportunity.

We went four and out in the first series. Everyone's head was down because we knew we were going to lose now.

Pigeon Forge took the field and went four and out as well.

The refs bring us back to the middle of the field and explain there will be another overtime until someone is declared the winner.

We win the toss again, but Coach decides to play defense first.

With everyone on the edge of their seats, we get Pigeon Forge to fourth down.

I knew by their formation what was coming. As soon as the quarterback snapped the ball, I came off the edge and met them both in the backfield. A host of bulldogs helped me wrestle them down.

Everyone starts to go crazy, but Scott is motioning for us to calm down.

The ref sets the ball back up and blows the whistle.

It is time for us to call a play and try to close this game out.

The first play Coach hands to Chonci and he is wrapped up after a couple yards. It's second down and goal with eight yards to go to win.

Coach calls Chonci's numbers again. He gets another couple yards. It's now third down and goal with six yards to pay dirt.

Coach calls a quarterback sneak with our Quarterback Rocky Blair. He drags the defensive players down to the one-yard line. The refs let him keep driving his feet until his forward progress has stopped. It's fourth down and inches. Coach signals a timeout to the refs.

We all ran over to the sideline. With all of us in the huddle, Coach makes eye contact with me and slightly nods his head. "Let's win this damn game boys. WOOOOOOOO!"

Scott looks everyone over and calls the play, "12!"

"1, 2, 3"

… "Bulldogs!"

We run out to the field, take our position, and wait for the refs to blow the whistle.

Rocky begins his cadence, "Down, set, hut, hut, hut."

He turns and hands the ball to me.

I drop my head and churn my legs as hard and fast as they will go.

Nothing Concealed: Veiled Secrecy Will Be Brought To Light

I hear the whistle blow. I turn my head sideways as I'm at the bottom of the domino stacked file of players. I see the ref run up, look down, and throw his hands up sternly with the field goal signal.

We won!

Bull horns, "Bad to the bone," and fans storm the field. I lay there and people just start piling on. I can't move or hear anything. I am pinned at the bottom of the pile until a hand fishes me out. Scott, with tears in his eyes, grabs me and says, "I love you!"

I start crying. I don't know why I am crying but the love that surrounded us all for winning is what I longed for.

Parents, fans, and players are all grabbing each other and crying joyous tears.

This lasts for fifteen or twenty minutes and Scott yells, "It's time Bean!"

They call everyone up to the middle and Scott hands Bean a pair of scissors. With tears in his eyes Bean cut that perfectly braided rattail, raised it high in the air, and we began to chant,

"Who are we?"

… "Bulldogs!"

"Who?"

… "Bulldogs!"

"1, 2, 3"

… "Bulldogs!"

Scott made his rounds back over to me, picked me up, squeezed me so hard, but never said a word. I cried happy tears hoping he never let me go.

That day, the grassy mountain was only a small ant hill. I confidently bounced up that hill when day one that mountain tackled me.

We all piled up in that two-toned brown Ford Aerostar van crying from the excitement of winning. I knew it was because football gave us all a glimmer of hope — that things could be different and that there is something worth working towards — that brought us hope in a time of hopelessness.

I found a true glimmer of hope in football. I found a glimmer of hope in my coach friend Scott Hill.

A few weeks later we had our season ending banquet. We all got dressed up in our finest Sunday best to pack the High School's cafeteria for food and awards.

There was so much excitement in the air. Kids buzzing from table to table like flies at a barbeque and all the parents full of smiles and laughs.

The banquet always had food, which was a plus because I got to eat and ignore all the old long-winded speakers talking about their past. I took my time to load up on every single free item: salads, baked potatoes, chicken breast, pork chops, gravy, and brownies. The sweet tea wasn't sweet at all so I did them a favor and unloaded as many packets of sugar I could find to create the necessary sweet tea.

As the night went on, more old people talked until Bean came to the podium. Scott followed a few paces behind and when they both arrived, everyone started screaming and applauding. It went until Bean raised his hand to hush the crowd.

This was one of the only times I hadn't seen him fired up. He expressed how much he loved all us boys and that's why he loved to coach.

Scott, still with an even bigger dip in his mouth leaned over to the mic and kept it short and sweet. "We did it and I love you boys."

Everyone erupted again screaming and chanting.

This is why I admired and loved Scott. He was a man of few words but they were always so impactful.

Once there was a quiet over the crowd, they started handing out awards.

I never really paid attention even though I always wanted to get recognized. They are both taking turns on handing out certain awards and explaining each with a back story of the kid that was receiving it.

I hear my name, "Jarrod, please stand up."

I slowly stand up. Scott grabs the mic and starts right in.

"This boy was fast as a hiccup and ain't scared of nothing. He always hustled to the ball and always wanted to win. I love him like my own and it is my pleasure to present Jarrod Houston with Mr. Hustle and the Headhunter award."

My eyes lit up and I started crying, not only because of the awards but because Scott said he loved me like one of his own. I walked slowly to the front while everyone clapped, and Scott handed me my awards. Before I went to sit back down, Scott grabbed me up and gave me the tightest hug and told me he loved me. I wanted for nothing more than to replay this season and this moment on infinite repeat.

I Am

"Kiss my ass you fuckin losers," as the ball went sailing over the fence smacking the rooftop.

A grey covered head popped out of the neighboring second story window in the cul-de-sac, "Who out there cussin?"

Ignoring her old ass hanging halfway out of the window and shaking her hand in disapproval, we go back to the final innings of the Sandlot World Series.

The sandlot was a fenced in field one of our friends' parents owned. In the sandlot we had intense baseball games and even worse bare-knuckle fights.

All the neighborhood kids would meet up on the weekends to stick their feet in to decide which team they were on.

"Bubble gum, bubble gum in a dish, how many pieces do you wish?"

I always argued my way into doing this chant to see who would be on teams.

"How many pieces do you wish," I would rush the person choosing. "Six."

"One, two, three, four, five, six," whoever's toe I landed on would be out and would go to the designated captains, who were usually me and Chonci.

"Bubble gum, bubble gum in a dish, how many pieces do you wish?" The next person, "four."

"One, two, three, four," and wherever my finger landed would be on my team. I would do this until everyone had enough players. If there was one extra, I would make them play on the team that had too many weak players. The weak players, I would explain while pointing them in the direction of the team they had to go, were either slow and couldn't hit the ball.

It was top of the seventh, when I smashed a dinger over the fence and let everyone know with my bat flip and "Kiss my ass you fuckin losers," when Ms. Sue popped out of the window like a jack-in-the-box.

Ms. Sue was an old, retired police officer that lived in our neighborhood and in our daily safe house because her grandson, Maurice, lived with her.

Mom didn't really like us going over there even though Ms. Sue was a retired police officer because her two oldest children had been in and out of jail so much, they had a permanent assigned bed at Jefferson County Jail, as I heard Mom say a few times. "Y'all go have fun but stay away from that damn Johnny." Johnny was Maurice's uncle that had sticky hands as Mom always said. "That nigger's hands stay with somebody else's property stuck to em."

Johnny was never a problem to me. He was a very large dark-skinned man but always threw the head and two fingers up when I saw him. The only thing I didn't like was how he always smelled like Listerine and outside.

Mom wouldn't let us walk around the block but would let us go to Ms. Sue's house and the sandlot because she could hear us arguing at one another clearly if she were to stand on the back porch or raise her bedroom window. We were close enough to hear her scream to get our asses home when we got the "food's ready" yell.

We kept playing. It's the top of the eighth inning and it's a guaranteed win for my team. Ms. Sue still has her body hanging out the window policing to hear of any other crimes and I'm back up to bat. I step back to take my practice swing, look at her in the window, and step up to the plate. The pitch comes right down the middle of the plate and I smack the laces off it. It goes flying over the fence. "HOME RUN BITCHES," as I'm staring at everyone in the field and bug-eyed look up at Ms. Sue.

Ms. Sue stretched her old leathery body even further out that widow and in her crackly smoked filled voice yelled, "I knew it was you, Jarrod!"

Laughing, I glanced up and she had disappeared out of the window and before I knew it, she was scuffing her house shoes along the concrete to the sandlots gate. Leaning on the sandlots gate with her house slides waving her skinny long wrinkled brown finger at me. "Get over here now!" Tough guy laughing, I knew I had better listen, so I started slowly walking towards her. Thinking to myself, she's old, there ain't nothing she can do to me with those brittle bones.

An arm's length away, her arm seemed to supernaturally stretch and, with pinpoint precision, her long wrinkly black pointer finger and thumb created a lasso. In a whipping motion that came from her elbow, she snagged the top of my ear. Like a mechanics clamp, her pointer finger and thumb fastened down on my ear and with each squeeze she lifted me higher off the ground. She had all the strength that caused her to be 65 years old stored in her thumb and pointer finger.

"Ouch, Ms. Sue!"

"I'll teach you to use that language over here, young man!" On my tiptoes, she kept yanking my ear harder and harder. Like a dog on a leash, she drug me up the street all the way until I looked up and saw the black shutters. She knocks on the door, Mom opens the door with her head down, "What did he do?"

My head is down and when I look up, Mom has two black and blue eyes. I drop my head back down as Ms. Sue then explains, "Your son was over on my property using foul language. I ask him to stop, and he continued to disrespect. Kathy, you know I won't stand for the disrespect."

Mom and Ms. Sue are looking eye to eye and no one seems to be phased by the two black eyes Mom lost in a boxing match with Dad.

"Sue, Jarrod isn't listening at home either and he is becoming difficult daily. I don't know what to do with him."

"Kathy, you know I can contact some of my old lieutenants and they can give him a tour of the facility because if he doesn't change, he'll end up there."

"I just don't know what's wrong with him."

With my ear still in the boney clutches of Ms. Sue, I can't help but to squirm because Mom is lying. She knows why I am acting like this. I wish Ms. Sue would say something to her about her eyes but they only transfer hands with my ear.

"I am sorry, Sue."

"It's ok, he can come back over if he cleans his mouth up."

Mom smacks me in the head with her opposite hand, "Tell her, Jarrod."

In a reluctant voice, "I am sorry, Sue."

"SUE, Jarrod!"

"I am sorry, Ms. Sue."

No sooner than the door closed, Mom started ranting. "Sue is worried about you cussing, Jarrod. She needs to worry about her raggedy ass kids in and out of jail."

In total agreement, I'm just shaking my head and without any notice a slap from the fiery pits of hell struck me directly on my mouth. I couldn't cry because the sneak attack knocked the tears to the back of my brain, causing a sensory malfunction. I couldn't do anything. It felt as though she slapped me with a glob full of Novocain.

That must've been Mom's final last straw, because after hitting me, Mom flopped down lifeless onto the blue corner sectional and the heaviest tears I'd ever seen or heard from her came flooding the room.

"Jarrod, I'm doing the best I can. Do you like getting in trouble?"

Mouth still numb from the thunderess slap, I just shake my head no.

"Why do you keep doing this to me? What have I done to you?"

"Me, Mom?" Look at your damn face. Dad hits you and whoops us, and this is my fault. Why are we still here? Why do you put up with Dad? Why don't you stand up for yourself like you always tell us to do?"

Tears flowing down her face, she sits up and slaps me again. Face still numb, I didn't flinch. This was my last straw.

"Mom, I hate Dad! I hate this house! I hate my life!"

Tears of anger start to flow down my face one at a time, "Leave Mom. Let's just leave."

"Jarrod, you don't understand. We can't. I'm afraid your dad will hurt me if we leave."

"Then let's go far far away and he'll never find us."

"It's not that easy, Jarrod."

"Yes, it is, Mom. We all hate this, and you know it."

My anger starts building and it dries up my tears.

"Maybe you deserve it then, Mom!"

Mom fights through the tears, stands up and places both her hands firmly on my arms. Talking through her teeth now, "SIT DOWN NOW."

She places me aggressively on the couch. Her voice changes and becomes soft, "Look at me, Jarrod." I look up at her, barely seeing her eyes through the swollenness, bruises, and tears. "Jarrod, promise me one thing. Promise me, you'll never hit a woman, especially your wife?" Aggressively she shakes me, "Say it, Jarrod."

"I will not hit a woman, especially my wife."

Now both of us crying again, Mom said, "Jarrod, you're a lot like your Dad because of your anger."

Nothing Concealed: Veiled Secrecy Will Be Brought To Light

At a young age, there was always one diss or comeback that would cause each of my siblings to go into a fit of rage and it was, "you're just like Dad." No matter what was going on, a fight, lying about eating the last of the snacks in the pantry, or just jugging on each other, this was the last-ditch effort diss to break down your opponent. This diss was always hundred percent when used.

I lost it.

"No, I'm not! I hate you, Mom! I hate everyone. When I'm old enough, I'm leaving and never coming back! You tell us to never live in fear but that's who you are Mom!"

I snatched away and ran outside. I didn't care about a whooping. I was walking until I could breathe again. The more I thought about what Mom said, the faster I walked, the faster I walked, the harder I cried. I walked until I couldn't walk anymore and just sat down in a field under a tree.

While sitting there I tried not to think but I couldn't. I hated everyone—my school, teachers, brothers, sister—and I didn't have any friends. Everyone said I was bad, so I guess that meant I was. When I got mad, I fought, destroying everything in my path until I felt better...until feeling better wore off.

Under the tree in total seclusion, I tried to cry but nothing came. The fear and rage inside me dried up all my tears.

The fear of being becoming Dad.

The fear of Dad.

The fear of what Dad might do.

The fear of going back home. Then after fear had run its course through my veins, anger surrounded me on all sides.

Anger because I was like Dad.

Anger because I hated everyone.

Anger because I hated myself.

Anger because no one wanted me.

Anger because I was Dad.

I was the mini-Hulk. Because I couldn't control my emotions, I destroyed whatever or whoever was in my path.

Anger because I was Mom.

I was Mom because I inherited the fear that drove her life. The fear of change and wanting something better for herself. The fear of being in control of her own life and not allowing Dad to control her every move. This was my life and nothing better was to come of it.

As I sat in that desolate field under that isolated tree, I began counting down the days until I would leave. I told myself, I wouldn't let Dad see me cry anymore and that when I had taken enough, I would kill him.

When was enough?

Peace

Finally, it was back: football! My parents realized I had become obsessed with the game of football so the constant threat in the house now was that if I got in any trouble then no football. This was my only motivation to stay on the straight and narrow. My parent's constant arguing and fighting didn't miss a beat, but now I had a way out: focus on football. I did everything to stay focused on football—collected trading cards, watched college and NFL games every week, played backyard football with my brothers and neighborhood kids, and watched old highlights of famous players. I had an obsessive behavior when it came to football because football understood me.

The season was finally upon us and, unlike the previous year of being timid before loading into the two-toned brown Ford Aerostar van, I was fully geared up waiting outside of those old rusty doors.

We pull up, van not even coming to a complete stop, the door slams open, and we hit the ground running. First ones there taking a knee at mid field eagerly waiting for coaches to arrive.

First Bean pulls up in his truck with "BBBB Bad to the Bone" blaring and following right behind him, Scott. Scott's arm half hanging out the window dancing to the music.

Yes, nothing has changed. I was right. They got out of the car with almost the identical clothes as the previous season minus Bean's rattail. The only thing missing was Scott's son wasn't accompanying him anymore.

Each league was run by age and weight. What that means is the youngest league was for 5–8-year-olds and if you were over one hundred and fifty pounds, in some cases you would have to move up to the older division. Scott's son fell in the first category, too old for the league, so now he was playing with the older boys. That explained his tardiness because he had to drop his son off at the upper fields for practice.

I sat on a knee, helmet on the ground, and hand on top of it anticipating what was next. What was next was the Scott Hill strut. Scott kind of leaned back when he walked, had a slight limp due to what he called "old knees," and he kind of swung his arms back and forth behind him as he walked. I could spot that strut from anywhere because I saw it all last season.

He struts up to us, puts his whistle in his mouth, blows it, and yells, "To the goal post!" Most kids hated conditioning, but I enjoyed beating everyone over and over to get the cheers from Scott.

I was more astute to the game of football than most of the kids now because it was my driving force and I consumed it like Halloween candy. It was my life and Scott realized that this year. He made me a captain and leaned on me to put other kids in their place on the field.

"Houston, this is your team now, so take control."

"Yes sir."

While last season, he called me son, he now called me Houston. It was an upgrade I took as a sign of respect. Whenever he called out Houston, I knew he was going to make a coaching comment and listen to me. I loved that he asked me questions, really processed them, unlike most adults who asked questions with the answer already made up in their minds.

"What the hell are you doing, Houston?"

"Why did you do that instead of what I told you to do?"

Listening to my fumbling reasoning, he would cock his head sideways and slightly nod. A brown spit followed by "Ok."

Even in those times I disobeyed, he would encourage me to explain so it made sense to him as well.

He loved me and I loved him.

From the past year's Superbowl win, things carried over. We hadn't lost a game and were destroying teams. We got so good the local Knoxville television stations would put us on their highlight reels. We were famous or at least everyone made us feel that way. You could've asked every kid on that field why we played so hard, and they would say we play for Bean and Scott. No matter how bad we beat a team, it didn't matter unless Scott and Bean brought us up together and told us how proud they were of us but that we needed to get better in a lot of areas on the field.

Nothing Concealed: Veiled Secrecy Will Be Brought To Light

"Boys, it don't matter how bad you beat somebody's ass unless you can find something to work on in that win."

"You gta fight for each other. You might fight and argue but you family boys."

We went undefeated and won our second consecutive Superbowl in style, on tv, with me getting MVP. I was living the high life for a seven-year-old.

Football has taught me that with every high moment in a game there will be a low moment but how you handle it determines who you truly are.

That low moment was about to happen in the fifth quarter of a game that I didn't know I was involved in.

How could I not see the changes?

How could I not notice that the man I so loved and admired was struggling like me? Maybe I didn't because coaching for him was like playing for me—an escape from reality that we hoped never ended.

Our downstairs basement is set up in my mind like an old-school polaroid picture.

FLASH, the picture is a still shot in my mind of the placement of everyone and everything around me. Mom was the person fanning the polaroid to accelerate the vintage snapshot of my emotions.

On the floor was a large wooden enclosed tv that didn't work but was simply a stand for the smaller tv to sit on it. Maybe Dad was a hoarder, or he thought eventually he would get it fixed but that's neither here nor there. Beside the smaller tv sat a beta machine, a VCR, a VCR rewind machine, two wooden towers with beta tapes and VHS tapes.

All three of my siblings were sitting around on the leopard print papasan chairs. There was a single papasan chair that caused arguments because if you claimed that chair you would be by yourself and not have to share the loveseat papasan where the remaining of us would have to smush together.

We would usually talk whoever had the single papasan into taking it out of its wicker chair and placing the leopard cushion on the ground allowing two people to sit on it so there wouldn't be so much human clutter on the loveseat. It would take a lot of coaxing but eventually it would happen.

Mom and Dad would hate this because they knew that those cushions on the ground would inevitably lead to an impromptu wrestling match that would no doubt lead to someone crying.

The cushion is on the ground and we're watching a movie. The musky aroma smell of the basement on that day stands out because a few days prior it had flooded from severe rains. The stench was overwhelming, and the basement was very dim, almost like an alley in a dark city street with dumpsters and only one light.

The inevitable happened and we were roughhousing. We hear the door at the top of the step briskly open. We had been warned not long before about wrestling, so it was a scramble to get the cushion and about face. Facing the opposite way to avoid eye contact, we just knew that the tongue lashing was coming followed by a whooping since we had clear instructions not to do what we were doing. Something was different in the air though.

Mom's walk and look was solemn, and she was very intentional about her movements walking towards us.

We hadn't heard any arguing today so what could have happened amidst our laughing and roughhousing? The closer Mom got the grimmer her demeanor became. We stood at attention awaiting, not knowing what was to come. Mom came closer, stood about five or six feet away and simply said, "Scott is dead."

I collapsed immediately to the ground and was consumed in tears of pain. My heart hurt. My stomach hurt. My head hurt. I just lay there and wept.

Why did Mom have to come tell me this?

What happened?

Everyone was stunned but no one reacted like me. Mom stood in confusion. She had always known how to console us when problems were inside the house, but this was out of her control.

I looked up and she was still standing there, not moving. I asked, "Why!"

Without hesitation, she sat us on the couch and started to give the hard facts of the cold case I asked about.

With tears streaming and Mom looking ghost-like, she explained without any sugar coating, "Scott killed himself."

"Killed himself?" I asked.

I knew what the words coming out of her mouth meant but didn't truly understand the gravity of them.

"What does that mean?"

Nothing Concealed: Veiled Secrecy Will Be Brought To Light

She explained that killing himself meant suicide and that he did in his truck with a shotgun, and that his son found him.

"Why, Why, Why, Why," with tears and snot streaming down my face. Mom knew but this is the evidence she would not divulge.

Mom went on to explain that killing yourself is a selfish act and that God will punish you for doing that. Selfish in the fact that you are only thinking about your pain and not how it will affect everyone else.

"A punishment from God and a life in hell is what you get for this selfish act."

I was terrified for Scott. All I could think of now was that I wanted to see him in heaven and I never will. I lay and wallow in my tears the rest of the day.

School was the next day but I just didn't have the power to get out of bed. All of me was drained. I just couldn't do it.

I lay in the bed hurt for two days. Everyone else got dressed and caught the bus as usual and I couldn't come to terms with how this was possible.

This god of a man loved me and showed me a way out through tough love coaching on a youth football field and everyone else carried on as though nothing happened. I was devastated. I remember Mom walking down those steps very gingerly the second day when everyone was gone. I knew it was to talk by her approach. She sat at the end of the bed and I just cried, not having any words.

"Baby, do you want to go to the funeral to pay your respects?"

I did nothing but lay there and cry.

Another adult hurt me, and I couldn't bring myself to look at him in that closed casket and face everyone else that would be there. I was angry at Scott for leaving me.

I was dumb for thinking his coaching and little league football would last forever.

I tried to explain it to Mom, but nothing came out except tears covered in every emotion.

Mom held me tighter as if she knew, she understood.

Before she got up, she left me with the most confusing message I have carried with me.

"He has peace now and can rest."

Just days prior she had said only hell awaits those that commit the selfish act of suicide. How come now it's "he's at peace and can rest?"

I pondered this daily now and I would carry it with me on the Jennings Route.

Standing

In the gloomy basement, I stood in solidarity as though I were in school for our daily Pledge of Allegiance. Head hung I mumbled, "I hope you never come back." I wanted him to hear me but in the same sense was terrified what would happen if he did.

Dad, clenching his jaw, turned his head swiftly around, "Look me in my eyes son."

Talking through his teeth, "I hope I don't either."

I was mortified, not by his response, but because he heard me.

He slammed the door behind him, never looking back.

I was consumed by the fear of "what if."

What if he doesn't come back and my Mom finds out?

Will she shun me?

What if he comes back and turns into the tornado of emotions, destroying everything in his path?

Will everyone find out I was the cold air that caused it?

It was a catch 22, so I stood paralyzed. Overtaken by the fear that surrounded me like the musky smell of the basement, I stood, feet planted for what felt like hours upon hours.

My mind swirling with thoughts and emotions about to erupt like a soda that had just been shaken.

I broke.

I fell to the papasan chair and silently whimpered.

I started pleading with God, "Why are you letting this happen and why does it have to be like this? Please make it all stop."

I was waiting for an answer.

I needed an answer now and it felt like a lifetime of waiting.

He didn't answer me.

I gathered myself like Dad would always coach by saying, "suck it up and wipe your eyes."

I did just that and headed outside as though nothing ever happened.

The day passed at a turtle pace. I tried to go to sleep early for a couple of reasons: one, to miss the interaction with Dad coming home from work and two, going to bed early always seemed to make time fast forward to the next day.

Weekends were always different in my household because Dad would wake everyone up no matter what time it was. He would say, "if I am up, everyone else needs to be up."

Anxiety still catches me if I am up on the weekend and no one else is.

On school days, we would have to get up a little after 5 a.m. every morning because there were so many of us to eat, share one bathroom, and catch the bus.

So why did Dad feel we needed to get up so early on the weekend?

Did we not earn a day to sleep in and enjoy the cool air under the warm covers?

I guess not, so like always, we complied, jumping to attention for the day's planned chores.

Each weekend, Dad would have us doing what I call adult jobs at such a young age because "we needed to learn how to use our hands."

Throughout the day, I could feel the tension radiating off Dad towards me. The first chore was edging the yard with the weed eater. This was always my job because Dad consistently commended me on how precise the lining was on the yard. Today was different. Jaw clenched, you could see the small muscle on his cheek protruding out as though he did strengthening exercises. "Jarrod!"

Without looking up, "Yes sir?"

"What are you doing?"

I wasn't trying to be smart, but the rhetorical question was only a set up, so I replied, "Edging the yard like you ask."

Dad never said anything about our interaction on his way to work the previous day, but I knew he hadn't forgotten. Maybe he finally understood what it felt like to hurt and be confused. I tried to tiptoe around everything he asked of me to not douse the flame of anger. It was inevitable, but I didn't want to be the one blamed during our late-night kid huddles reviewing the day.

"That's not how I showed you how to hold the weed eater."

I knew it was a setup but what was I supposed to say, "No?" Absolutely not.

Without looking up, I changed the positioning of the weed eater facing downward and started back edging along the sidewalk.

There was a certain method he wanted every time: a two-to-three-inch gap between the sidewalk and the grass and for it to be to the dirt. This method never made sense to me, but your wish is my command is all I could think.

As I started back along the path, he yells my name again, "Jarrod!"

I look up in apprehension. I couldn't really hear him with the noise of the lawnmower and weed eater, but I could read all the Ebonics sign language he was gesturing at me.

I dropped the weed eater and ran to him.

Dad would always say, "Put some pep in yo step when I call your name," so it was an all-out sprint up that sidewalk to reach him.

I finally reach him at the top of the steps. Standing in fear with my head hanging low, he begins to point out everything that is not to his liking.

I never looked up at him and I think this infuriated him even more. He grabbed me by my face, thumb, and pointer finger on each side of my jaw, squeezing as if he were trying to get the last drop of juice out of an orange.

I immediately start crying, which seemed to anger him more. I am crying, he is squeezing, but we both know why this is happening.

It had nothing to do with my lawn care performance but everything to do with our altercation from the previous day.

He was proving his point by scaring me straight. He obviously didn't care about my feelings because I hurt his, and he was just looking for an opportunity to get even.

My brothers both seeing what happened never missed a beat in their lawn care responsibilities, but knew I had crossed Dad somehow.

I don't blame them for not coming to my aid, because why should everyone be punished for one man's mistake?

"You had better stop crying or ima give you something to cry about."

By this time, I was full on crocodile tears and there wasn't enough fear to scare those tears dry.

He snatches me by my hand and leads me down the steps around the side of the house. I can only remember thinking how glad I was not to have him looking at me with those piercing eyes.

I knew what was coming, but at a young age I realized pain is temporary and the whooping would only last until his anger was gone. I just had to prepare myself for the worst beating and know it would be over soon.

With him squeezing the life out of my right wrist with his left hand, almost like a ninja he took his belt off with his left hand.

We both made eye contact for a millisecond so as to prepare, and it began.

He hit me wherever the belt landed, and I knew he felt the payback pleasure.

The first few angry strokes, I didn't cry but the further the belt climbed up my back the yelps crept out. With every word he said, the belt struck me somewhere different along my body.

"DIDN'T I TELL YOU!"

"DIDN'T I TELL YOU!"

"DIDN'T I TELL YOU!"

I was compelled to silence because we both knew this wasn't over my weed eating technique.

It went until Dad got out all his anger. He snatched my right arm higher, informed me, "You better suck it up and get back to work now!"

Sniffling with my head hung, I ran back to my work post.

The entire time my brothers knew what was taking place, but the sounds of the lawnmower drowned out my screams, so they stayed the course.

We worked and worked until the task was done to Dad's liking.

Now, we waited for the next task on the agenda.

During our lunch break, my brothers would check on me with roaming eyes and head nods, to not tip off or anger the foreman.

Dusk was upon us, and that's when our day usually would end. It was the part of the day we enjoyed because we could be kids, whether it be hide-n-seek, Nintendo, or just backyard football. We would indulge until Mom yelled out her window, "Boys, it's time to come in!"

Once we had loitered for a minute too long, Mom yelled again, "Boys, don't make me come out and get y'all's asses!"

Nothing Concealed: Veiled Secrecy Will Be Brought To Light

Dad called me in the house to give me "the speech." "The speech" happened when Dad realized he took things too far but still wanted to justify his actions with some deep and profound explanation.

It usually went like this, "Son, I love you, but you have to realize it hurts me more than it does you, to spank you. Son, I didn't have a Dad around that loved me enough to discipline me and expect my best daily. I hold you to a higher standard because I'm teaching you to be strong independent men."

I wanted to say, "I hate you and wish you would leave," but instead I chose silence with alligator tears ready at any moment to drown in my emotions.

I was at my wit's end.

Dad hates me, Scott isn't here anymore, and the house still feels like a war zone. The babysitters are becoming bolder in their actions and I don't know what to do anymore.

Mom and Dad always say, "Kids don't have stress because they eat, sleep, and shit for free."

They were so wrapped up in their momentary struggles, they forgot what it was like to be a kid. Mom and Dad forgot about everyone and everything else, besides themselves.

I had a plan.

Mom said Scott had peace because he was no longer in this world.

What if I sought that same peace Scott found?

I knew I couldn't go anywhere unless it was approved first by my parents and the one place that always seemed to be open was the Jennings' route.

I lay in bed that night thinking about what peace felt like and how I would find it.

Would everything just go numb?

Was there happiness after this?

How could I find peace?

Was peace more time?

Was it freedom from rules?

Why was the thought of peace so scary?

The next morning, I got up as though nothing had taken place the previous day.

With plan in mind, I asked Mom if I could run the Jennings' route.

Mom agreed immediately without hesitation.

My plan was as tight as the laces I pulled in my shoes.

I walked outside as normal to the starting line, the mailbox.

To not be obvious, I started our formulaic stretches starting with the hang and hold. I bounced a few times touching my toes, stood up, and took a deep breath.

Before leaving, whoever was running would give a yell just to let Mom and Dad know because there was sort of an estimated time clock. If you weren't back by then, they would allot a few more minutes, then the search party would be deployed.

My feet take off, bouncing off the pavement up Hilltop drive making my way to Rankin street. At the stop sign, I take the left down the hill on Chucky Pike.

My mind is spiraling but I'm prepared.

Approaching the next stop sign, I yield to look both ways and sprint across the street. I'm on the Jennings' route and, before you know it, my plan is unfolding. Now, at my destination my run slows down to a slow walk.

My heart begins racing and a lump in my throat develops.

Lump in my throat and my heart beating a record pace, I continue to walk without thinking.

Everything became eerily desolate as I approached my target destination: the bridge.

The lump in my throat has been replaced with the thumping of my heartbeat. I tried to swallow to get it back down to my chest, but I had no saliva to move it.

I peep over the bridge and get an uneasy feeling in my stomach, but I knew what the plan was.

All I can think about is finding that peace Scott had and knowing this is the only way.

I baby step closer and place my hand on the two-toned painted bridge.

I run my hand slowly along the top of the concrete and can feel the chipped paint crumble and fall.

Terrified, I can now hear my heart beating in my eardrums with a heavy deep beat.

Nothing Concealed: Veiled Secrecy Will Be Brought To Light

BOOM BOOM BOOM BOOM is all I can hear as I look over and see Mossy Creek flowing below.

My mind kept saying, "You here now, so no turning back."

I take another quick glance over and tears begin flowing uncontrollably down my face. No sound came out but the tears were like a waterfall of release. Release from the hurt and pain. Release from the anger. Release from hopelessness. PEACE.

I place one hand firmly to brace for my first foot to step up.

I am here.

I am ready.

I get the next foot up on the bridge. Now, I am standing erect atop the bridge looking down as Mossy Creek rushes beneath.

The stillness was ear-piercing.

Encouraging myself mentally, "Jarrod you can do this, and it'll all be better soon."

Standing there for God only knows how long, I started to sway.

Just when I composed my nerves with all the self-coaxing, I heard a small voice in the distance, "Jarrod what are you doing?"

It was Chunky aka Chonci. I called him Chunky from a young age because his name used to be so hard to pronounce.

He must have needed a break from jail as well and knew the Jennings' route was the sure-fire getaway.

I slightly turn my head, and Chunky, without missing a revolution, rode right past me, never looking at me.

Maybe he was thinking the same thing on his previous Jennings routes? Either way, the stoicism in his bike postured lean and his voice caused me to lose all intentions and step down immediately.

I stepped down. Now, frozen from the neck down, only turning my head to look out into the rapidly moving Mossy creek, I broke again.

I stood there sobbing. I looked for Chunky but he disappeared around the bend of the route. I couldn't scream for him to come back and I couldn't move.

It was complete stillness besides the tears flowing down my face. I needed someone but it was just me, alone again.

My tears must have floated me back to Hilltop Drive because when I looked up, I was staring at the black shutters on the house. Shortly thereafter, I saw Chunky riding up and we had a very business professional exchange. I don't know if he thought I was just being the mischievous Jarrod he knew me to be or if he was stopping me from hurting myself. Either way, we walked past each other, no words spoken, but body language understanding this was to never be spoken of again.

Many times I cried, it was like a dam releasing water. Once the overflow of water was released by the dam's walls, water height would level out, allowing normalcy again.

This was different. I got the tears out but the built-up pain I carried onto the bridge stayed with me and felt even heavier now.

This heaviness I would carry with me every moment for the rest of my life.

The Jennings' route still stands in our household but understanding the many facets it served never will.

Lightning Source UK Ltd.
Milton Keynes UK
UKHW022253200123
415719UK00015B/109